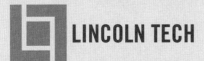

LINCOLN TECH

# Lincoln Technical Institute
# Tasksheet Manual

## VOLUME 3

JONES & BARTLETT
LEARNING

*World Headquarters*
Jones & Bartlett Learning
5 Wall Street
Burlington, MA 01803
978-443-5000
info@jblearning.com
www.jblearning.com

Jones & Bartlett Learning books and products are available through most bookstores and online booksellers. To contact Jones & Bartlett Learning directly, call 800-832-0034, fax 978-443-8000, or visit our website, www.jblearning.com.

978-1284-16483-1

**Production Credits**
General Manager: Kimberly Brophy
VP, Product Development: Christine Emerton
Product Manager: Jesse Mitchell
Product Owner: Kevin Murphy
Senior Vendor Manager: Sara Kelly
Marketing Manager: Amanda Banner
Manufacturing and Inventory Control Supervisor: Amy Bacus
Composition and Project Management: Integra Software Services Pvt. Ltd.
Cover Design: Scott Moden
Director of Rights & Media: Joanna Gallant
Rights & Media Specialist: Robert Boder
Media Development Editor: Shannon Sheehan
Cover Image (Title Page): © Umberto Shtanzman/Shutterstock
Printing and Binding: McNaughton & Gunn
Cover Printing: McNaughton & Gunn

**Library of Congress Cataloging-in-Publication Data**


6048

Printed in the United States of America

22 21 20    10 9 8 7 6 5 4

# Contents

▶ **TASK** Research vehicle service information including vehicle service history, service precautions, and technical service bulletins.

**MAST**
8A2

Time off_____

Time on_____

Total time_____

**CDX Tasksheet Number: C387**

1. **Using the VIN for identification, use the appropriate source to access the vehicle's service history in relation to prior related engine management work or customer concerns.**

    a. **List any related repairs/concerns, and their dates:**

2. **Using the VIN for identification, access any relevant technical service bulletins for the particular vehicle you are working on in relation to engine management updates or other service issues.**

    a. **List any related service bulletins (bulletin number and title):**

3. **Have your supervisor/instructor verify satisfactory completion of this procedure, any observations found, and any necessary action(s) recommended.**

**Performance Rating**

**CDX Tasksheet Number: C387**

| 0 | 1 | 2 | 3 | 4 |
|---|---|---|---|---|
|   |   |   |   |   |

Supervisor/instructor signature _____ Date _____

▶ **TASK** Demonstrate the use of the three Cs
(concern, cause, and correction).

**Additional Task**

Time off_____

Time on_____

Total time_____

**CDX Tasksheet Number: N/A**

1. Using the following scenario, write up the three Cs as listed on most repair orders. Assume that the customer authorized the recommended repairs.

   A vehicle has been brought to your shop with an engine performance/driveability concern. The customer tells you that the vehicle used to run rough only when accelerating up a hill but now it is running rough when accelerating even lightly. The MIL light also blinks when the engine is running rough. The customer thought it was bad gas, but after that tank ran out, the customer refilled it with good gas from a very reputable station and it still runs rough even after using half a tank. The customer authorizes your shop to perform a diagnosis and you find the following:

   a. P0305—Engine misfire on cylinder #5.
   b. #5 spark plug boot is leaking high voltage to the cylinder head under light load.
   c. All of the spark plugs are moderately worn.
   d. All of the spark plug wires are original. The vehicle is about 8 years old and has nearly 100,000 miles on it.
   e. Cylinder relative compression is within specifications.
   f. The air filter is dirty.
   g. The oil change is almost 1000 miles and 2 months overdue.
   h. The oil seals and gaskets look to be in good shape with no leaks.
   i. The water pump seal is starting to seep coolant and the coolant is a bit dirty.
   j. The belts look like they have been replaced recently.

   > **NOTE** Ask your instructor whether you should use a copy of the shop repair order or the three Cs below to record this information.

2. **Concern/complaint:**

3. **Cause:**

4. **Correction:**

5. Other recommended service:

6. Have your supervisor/instructor verify satisfactory completion of this procedure, any observations found, and any necessary action(s) recommended.

**Performance Rating**

CDX Tasksheet Number: N/A

| | | | | |
|---|---|---|---|---|
| 0 | 1 | 2 | 3 | 4 |

Supervisor/instructor signature _____ Date _____

▶ **TASK** Identify and interpret engine performance concerns; determine needed action.

**MAST**
**8A1**

**CDX Tasksheet Number: C386**

1. **List the customer concern:**

2. **Research the particular concern in the appropriate service information.**

   a. **List the possible causes:**

3. **Inspect the engine and management system to determine the cause of the concern.**

   a. **List the steps you took to determine the fault and the result for each step:**

4. **List the cause of the concern/complaint:**

5. **List the necessary action(s) to correct this fault:**

6. Have your supervisor/instructor verify satisfactory completion of this procedure, any observations found, and any necessary action(s) recommended.

**Performance Rating**

CDX Tasksheet Number: C386

| 0 | 1 | 2 | 3 | 4 |
|---|---|---|---|---|

Supervisor/instructor signature _____ Date _____

**MAST**
**8C4**

Time off_____

Time on_____

Total time_____

**CDX Tasksheet Number: C422**

**Vehicle used for this activity:**

Year _____ Make _____ Model_____

Odometer_____ VIN_____

1. **Research the fuel filter replacement procedure for this vehicle in the appropriate information.**

   a. **List any special procedures and/or tools to perform this task:**

   b. **Look up the flat rate time for this task:** _____ **hr**

2. **Release any fuel pressure in the system by following the manufacturer's recommended procedure.**

3. **Follow the specified procedure to remove the fuel filter.**

4. **Have your supervisor/instructor verify removal of the fuel filter. Supervisor's/instructor's initials:** _____

5. **Install a new fuel filter (or reinstall the old one if your instructor directed you to do so).**

6. **Once the filter is installed correctly, clean up any spilled fuel and dispose of it properly.**

7. **Apply the vehicle's parking brake and secure the vehicle with wheel chocks to prevent the vehicle from rolling.**

8. **Turn the ignition switch to run and check for any fuel leaks. Immediately shut off the vehicle if a leak is present. Repair any leaks.**

   **NOTE** Ask your supervisor/instructor whether or not to perform the next action before proceeding.

9. **Cut the old filter open with a hacksaw to examine the inside. List what you found inside the filter:**

10. Have your supervisor/instructor verify satisfactory completion of this
procedure, any observations found, and any necessary action(s) recommended.

**Performance Rating**

**CDX Tasksheet Number: C422**

| | | | | |
|---|---|---|---|---|
| ☐ | ☐ | ☐ | ☐ | ☐ |
| 0 | 1 | 2 | 3 | 4 |

Supervisor/instructor signature _____ Date _____

Inspect and test fuel pump(s) and pump control system for pressure, regulation, and volume; perform needed action.

**MAST**
**8D3**

**CDX Tasksheet Number: C868**

1. Research the following specifications/procedures for this vehicle in the appropriate service information.

   a. List the type of fuel pump that is used in this vehicle: _____
   b. Fuel pump pressure (key on/engine off): _____ psi/kPa
   c. Fuel pump pressure (key on/engine idling): _____ psi/kPa
   d. Fuel pump pressure (deadhead): _____ psi/kPa
   e. Fuel pump volume: pt/L/oz/lb per: _____ sec/min/hr
   f. List the steps to relieve the pressure in the fuel system:

2. Have your supervisor/instructor verify your answers. Supervisor's/instructor's initials: _____

3. Test the fuel pump according to the specified procedure and list your observations.

   a. Fuel pump pressure (key on/engine off): _____ psi/kPa
   b. Fuel pump pressure (key on/engine idling): _____ psi/kPa
   c. Fuel pump pressure (deadhead): _____ psi/kPa
   d. Fuel pump volume: _____ pt/L/oz/lb per: _____ sec/min/hr
   e. Does the system hold pressure for at least 5 minutes once the key is turned off? Yes: _____ No: _____

   > **NOTE** Keep the fuel in the container for the next task, C420: Check fuel for contaminants; determine needed action.

4. Determine any necessary action(s):

5. Have your supervisor/instructor verify your conclusions. Supervisor's/instructor's initials: _____

6. Perform any necessary actions as approved by your supervisor/instructor and list the results here:

7. **Have your supervisor/instructor verify satisfactory completion of this procedure, any observations found, and any necessary action(s) recommended.**

**CDX Tasksheet Number: C868**

| 0 | 1 | 2 | 3 | 4 |
|---|---|---|---|---|
| ☐ | ☐ | ☐ | ☐ | ☐ |

Supervisor/instructor signature _____ Date _____

**CDX Tasksheet Number: C420**

1. **Obtain a quantity of fuel from the vehicle into the fuel container.**

> **NOTE** This is best done while performing a fuel pump volume test.

2. **Pour 90 mL of gasoline into the graduated test tube.**

3. **Let this settle for a minute or two. Observe any contaminants in the fuel. List your observations:**

4. **Add 10 mL of water, bringing the total volume to 100 mL.**

5. **Cap the test tube tightly with a cork or other appropriate device.**

> **NOTE** Be sure you hold the cap firmly in place during this procedure. It will become pressurized, which could force the cap off, spraying fuel a considerable distance.

6. **Slowly and carefully agitate the fuel/water mix for 30 seconds to bring the water into contact with the fuel. If there is any alcohol in the fuel, this will allow the water to be absorbed by the alcohol.**

7. **Allow the mixture to settle for a minute or two. Observe the level of the water in the bottom of the test tube. Anything higher than the initial 10 mL is the amount of alcohol in the fuel. List your observation(s):**

8. **Determine any necessary action(s):**

9. **Have your supervisor/instructor verify your observations. Supervisor's/ instructor's initials: _____**

10. **Carefully pour off the fuel in the test tube back to the fuel container. Make sure no water leaves the test tube.**

11. **Properly dispose of the remaining water/fuel mixture.**

12. Have your supervisor/instructor verify satisfactory completion of this procedure, any observations found, and any necessary action(s) recommended.

**Performance Rating**

CDX Tasksheet Number: C420

| 0 | 1 | 2 | 3 | 4 |
|---|---|---|---|---|

Supervisor/instructor signature _____ Date _____

Time off_____

Time on_____

Total time_____

**CDX Tasksheet Number: C842**

**Vehicle used for this activity:**

Year _____ Make _____ Model_____

Odometer_____ VIN_____

1. Research the fuel injector testing procedure for this vehicle in the appropriate service information. List the following:

   a. Specified resistance for the fuel injectors: _____ ohms
   b. Fuel pump pressure (key on/engine off): _____ psi/kPa
   c. List or print off and attach to this sheet the steps to test the fuel injectors.

2. Visually inspect the fuel injectors for leaks, damage, etc. List your observations:

3. Follow the specified procedure to test the fuel injectors. List your observations:

4. If the service information doesn't list a method for testing the injectors, use the following method.

   a. Install the fuel pressure gauge on the fuel rail.
   b. Disconnect the fuel injector electrical connectors.
   c. Connect the injector pulsing tool to one fuel injector, according to the toolmaker's instructions, and set it for the specified amount of time in milliseconds.
   d. Pressurize the fuel rail by turning on the ignition switch for a few seconds. Then turn the ignition switch off.
   e. List the fuel pressure: _____ psi/kPa
   f. Activate the injector pulsing tool for the appropriate amount of time. Watch the pressure gauge and record the pressure after the injector has been cycled on and off (one time). List your readings below. Continue this test on each fuel injector, remembering to pressurize the fuel rail each time before activating the injector pulsing tool.

g. **List your readings for each injector.**

Injector #1 _____ psi/kPa   Injector #2 _____ psi/kPa
Injector #3 _____ psi/kPa   Injector #4 _____ psi/kPa
Injector #5 _____ psi/kPa   Injector #6 _____ psi/kPa
Injector #7 _____ psi/kPa   Injector #8 _____ psi/kPa

> **NOTE** Uneven pressure drops indicate uneven fuel flow through each injector.

5. **Determine any necessary action(s):**

6. **Measure the resistance of each fuel injector and list your readings.**

Injector #1 _____ Ohms   Injector #2 _____ Ohms
Injector #3 _____ Ohms   Injector #4 _____ Ohms
Injector #5 _____ Ohms   Injector #6 _____ Ohms
Injector #7 _____ Ohms   Injector #8 _____ Ohms

7. **Determine any necessary action(s):**

8. **Have your supervisor/instructor verify satisfactory completion of this procedure, any observations found, and any necessary action(s) recommended.**

**Performance Rating**

**CDX Tasksheet Number: C842**

| 0 | 1 | 2 | 3 | 4 |
|---|---|---|---|---|
|   |   |   |   |   |

Supervisor/instructor signature _____ Date _____

**MAST**
8D1

Time off_____

Time on_____

Total time_____

**CDX Tasksheet Number: C713**

**Vehicle used for this activity:**

Year _____ Make _____ Model_____

Odometer_____ VIN_____

1. **List the fuel injection system-related customer concern:**

2. **Verify the concern and list your observations here:**

3. **Research the possible causes for this concern in the appropriate service information.**

   a. **List or print off and attach to this sheet the possible causes:**

   b. **List or print off and attach to this sheet the procedure for diagnosing the concern:**

4. **Follow the specified procedure to diagnose the concern. List your tests and results here:**

5. **List the cause of the concern:**

6. Determine any necessary action(s) to correct the fault:

7. Have your supervisor/instructor verify satisfactory completion of this procedure, any observations found, and any necessary action(s) recommended.

**Performance Rating**

| 0 | 1 | 2 | 3 | 4 |
|---|---|---|---|---|

Supervisor/instructor signature _____ Date _____

**CDX Tasksheet Number: C962**

1. **Research the procedure and specifications for servicing the air filter, housing, and ductwork in the appropriate service information.**

    a. **Specified air filter number:** _____

2. **Following the specified procedure, remove the air filter from the filter housing.**

3. **Inspect the air filter and list the condition:**

4. **Inspect the filter housing and ductwork. List your observations:**

5. **Clean the filter housing following the specified procedure.**

6. **Have your supervisor/instructor verify removal. Supervisor's/instructor's initials:** _____

7. **Following the specified procedure, reinstall the air filter, housing, and ductwork.**

8. **Have your supervisor/instructor verify satisfactory completion of this procedure, any observations found, and any necessary action(s) recommended.**

**Performance Rating**

**CDX Tasksheet Number: C962**

| 0 | 1 | 2 | 3 | 4 |
|---|---|---|---|---|

Supervisor/instructor signature _____ Date _____

Inspect throttle body, air induction system, intake manifold, and gaskets for vacuum leaks and/or unmetered air.

**MAST**
**8D6**

Time off_____

Time on_____

Total time_____

**CDX Tasksheet Number: C424**

**Vehicle used for this activity:**

Year _____ Make _____ Model_____

Odometer_____ VIN_____

1. **Visually inspect the air induction system for any obvious leaks such as cracks, loose fittings, or missing hoses. List your observations:**

2. **Use an appropriate leak detection tool to test for any non-obvious leaks and/or unmetered air. List your tests and observations:**

3. **Determine any necessary action(s):**

4. **Have your supervisor/instructor verify satisfactory completion of this procedure, any observations found, and any necessary action(s) recommended.**

© 2019 Jones & Bartlett Learning, LLC, an Ascend Learning Company

**Performance Rating**

**CDX Tasksheet Number: C424**

| 0 | 1 | 2 | 3 | 4 |
|---|---|---|---|---|

Supervisor/instructor signature _____ Date _____

**MAST**
**8D8**

**CDX Tasksheet Number: C665**

**Vehicle used for this activity:**

Year _____ Make _____ Model_____

Odometer_____ VIN_____

1.  **List the idle speed control-related customer concern:**

2.  **Research and list the desired idle speed:** _____ **rpm**

3.  **Research the particular concern in the appropriate service information and list the possible causes:**

4.  **Using the specified procedure, verify the vehicle idle speed and list here:** _____ **rpm**

5.  **Using the specified procedure, test the idle control system operation. List your test(s) observation(s) here:**

6.  **Determine any necessary action(s):**

7.  **Return the vehicle to its beginning condition and return any tools you used to their proper locations.**

8. Have your supervisor/instructor verify satisfactory completion of this procedure, any observations found, and any necessary action(s) recommended.

**Performance Rating**

**CDX Tasksheet Number: C665**

| | | | | |
|---|---|---|---|---|
| 0 | 1 | 2 | 3 | 4 |

Supervisor/instructor signature _____ Date _____

Inspect the integrity of the exhaust manifold, exhaust pipes, muffler(s), catalytic converter(s), resonator(s), tail pipe(s), and heat shields; perform needed action.

**MAST**
8D9

Time off_____

Time on_____

Total time_____

**CDX Tasksheet Number: C428**

1. **Safely raise and secure the vehicle on a hoist.**

2. **Inspect the following parts for damage, wear, or missing components. Also, check the integrity of the pipes by squeezing them with the large arc joint pliers. List your observations about each.**

   a. **Exhaust manifold(s):**

   b. **Exhaust pipes:**

   c. **Muffler(s):**

   d. **Catalytic converter(s):**

   e. **Resonator(s):**

   f. **Tail pipe(s):**

   g. **Heat shield(s):**

© 2019 Jones & Bartlett Learning, LLC, an Ascend Learning Company

3. Determine any necessary action(s):

4. Have your supervisor/instructor verify your conclusions. Supervisor's/instructor's initials: _____

5. Perform any necessary actions as approved by your supervisor/instructor. List them here:

6. Have your supervisor/instructor verify satisfactory completion of this procedure, any observations found, and any necessary action(s) recommended.

**Performance Rating**

CDX Tasksheet Number: C428

| 0 | 1 | 2 | 3 | 4 |
|---|---|---|---|---|

Supervisor/instructor signature _____ Date _____

© 2019 Jones & Bartlett Learning, LLC, an Ascend Learning Company

▶ **TASK** Inspect condition of exhaust system hangers, brackets, clamps, and heat shields; determine needed action.

**MAST**
**8D10**

Time off_____

Time on_____

Total time_____

**CDX Tasksheet Number: C963**

1. Safely raise and secure the vehicle on a hoist.

2. Inspect the following parts for damage, wear, or missing components. Also, check the integrity of the pipes by squeezing them with the large arc joint pliers. List your observations about each.

   a. Exhaust system hangers, brackets, and clamps:

   b. Heat shields:

3. Determine any necessary action(s):

4. Have your supervisor/instructor verify your conclusions. Supervisor's/instructor's initials: time _____

5. Perform any necessary actions as approved by your supervisor/instructor. List them here:

6. Have your supervisor/instructor verify satisfactory completion of this procedure, any observations found, and any necessary action(s) recommended.

© 2019 Jones & Bartlett Learning, LLC, an Ascend Learning Company

**Performance Rating**

**CDX Tasksheet Number: C963**

| 0 | 1 | 2 | 3 | 4 |
|---|---|---|---|---|
|   |   |   |   |   |

Supervisor/instructor signature _____ Date _____

Perform exhaust system back-pressure test;
determine needed action.

Time off_____

Time on_____

Total time_____

**CDX Tasksheet Number: C429**

1. Research the procedure to test exhaust back-pressure on this vehicle in the appropriate service information.

    a. List the location for installing the back-pressure gauge: _____

    b. List the maximum allowable back-pressure: _____ in/hg or psi/kPa at _____ rpm

2. Install the back-pressure gauge according to the specified procedure.

3. Measure the exhaust back-pressure, being careful to follow the specified procedure.

    a. List your readings obtained: _____ in/hg or psi/kPa at _____ rpm

4. Determine any necessary action(s):

5. Have your supervisor/instructor verify satisfactory completion of this procedure, any observations found, and any necessary action(s) recommended.

**Performance Rating**

CDX Tasksheet Number: C429

| 0 | 1 | 2 | 3 | 4 |
|---|---|---|---|---|

Supervisor/instructor signature _____ Date _____

Test the operation of turbocharger/supercharger systems;
determine needed action.

**MAST**
**8D13**

Time off_____

Time on_____

Total time_____

**CDX Tasksheet Number: C869**

**Vehicle used for this activity:**

Year _____ Make _____ Model _____

Odometer _____ VIN _____

> **NOTE** This task is extremely hazardous and should be performed only under close supervisor/instructor supervision. Diagnosis of this fault may require test driving the vehicle on the school grounds or on a hoist, both of which carry severe risks. Attempt this task only with full permission from your supervisor/instructor and follow all the guidelines and laws exactly.

1. **Research the testing and specifications for this vehicle in the appropriate service information.**

   a. **Maximum boost: _____ psi/kPa**
   b. **List, or print off and attach to this sheet, the procedure for testing the turbocharger/supercharger:**



   c. **Have your supervisor/instructor approve the specifications and testing procedure. Supervisor's/instructor's initials: _____**

2. **Following the specified procedure, test the turbocharger/supercharger. List your tests and results:**



3. **Determine any necessary action(s):**



4. **Have your supervisor/instructor verify satisfactory completion of this procedure, any observations found, and any necessary action(s) recommended.**

**Performance Rating**

**CDX Tasksheet Number: C869**

| 0 | 1 | 2 | 3 | 4 |
|---|---|---|---|---|

Supervisor/instructor signature _____ Date _____

**MAST**
8D12

Time off_____

Time on_____

Total time_____

**CDX Tasksheet Number: C965**

**Vehicle used for this activity:**

Year _____ Make _____ Model_____

Odometer_____ VIN_____

1. **On a diesel vehicle equipped with diesel exhaust fluid, research the following specifications in the appropriate service information.**

   a. **Specified diesel exhaust fluid:** _____

   b. **Specified replenishment interval:** _____ **mi/km/mo**

   c. **Specified diesel fluid tank capacity:** _____

   d. **Specified urea content:** _____ **% or specific gravity**

   e. **List the purpose of diesel exhaust fluid:** _____

2. **Following the specified procedure, obtain and measure the urea content or specific gravity of the DEF fluid. List your results:**

3. **Check the level of diesel exhaust fluid in the reservoir. List your observations:**

4. **If necessary, refill the diesel exhaust fluid to the proper level.**

5. **Have your supervisor/instructor verify satisfactory completion of this procedure, any observations found, and any necessary action(s) recommended.**

**Performance Rating**

**CDX Tasksheet Number: C965**

| 0 | 1 | 2 | 3 | 4 |
|---|---|---|---|---|
|   |   |   |   |   |

Supervisor/instructor signature _____ Date _____

▶ **TASK** Diagnose emission and driveability concerns caused by catalytic converter system; determine needed action.

**MAST**
**8E9**

Time off_____

Time on_____

Total time_____

**CDX Tasksheet Number: C714**

1. **Research the catalytic converter testing procedure for this vehicle in the appropriate service information.**

   a. **List or print off and attach to this sheet the procedure to test the converter:**

   b. **If no procedure is available, there are four generally accepted methods of testing a converter:**

      1. **The first is a pre-catalyst/post-catalyst emission test (sometimes called an intrusive or intrusion test).**
      2. **The second is a cylinder ignition-shorting emission test where one cylinder's ignition is disabled and the resulting emissions are measured and compared to the pre-shorted emission readings.**
      3. **On OBDII-equipped vehicles, using the pre-catalyst and post-catalyst $O_2$ sensor readings to show a difference in exhaust oxygen content will indicate converter efficiency.**
      4. **Using mode 6 data from the vehicle's PCM to indicate the number of failure counts for the catalyst**
         **Ask your supervisor/instructor which method to use, and list it here: _____**

   > **NOTE** Some local regulatory authorities mandate a loaded cruise test. This test is hard to duplicate in most shops and is best done on a dynamometer. Unless your shop has this piece of equipment available, it would be best not to perform a loaded cruise test. Also, in some states a no-load cruise test is allowed on certain vehicles. Please note that some vehicles can experience transmission failure if this test is performed. Therefore, we do not recommend performing this test on any vehicle unless it is with your supervisor's/instructor's direct authorization and supervision.

2. **Test the catalytic converter following the specified procedure. List your tests and observations:**

3. **Determine any necessary action(s):**

4. Have your supervisor/instructor verify satisfactory completion of this procedure, any observations found, and any necessary action(s) recommended.

**Performance Rating**

CDX Tasksheet Number: C714

| 0 | 1 | 2 | 3 | 4 |
|---|---|---|---|---|

Supervisor/instructor signature _____ Date _____

Diagnose emissions and driveability concerns caused by the evaporative emissions control (EVAP) system; determine needed action.

**MAST**
**8E5**

**CDX Tasksheet Number: C844**

**Vehicle used for this activity:**

Year _____ Make _____ Model_____

Odometer_____ VIN_____

1. **List the customer concern:**

2. **Research the particular concern in the appropriate service information.**

   a. **List the possible causes:**

   b. **List or print off and attach to this sheet the procedure for diagnosing the concern:**

3. **Using the recommended procedure, inspect and diagnose any emissions and driveability concerns caused by the evaporative emissions control system. List your tests and observations here:**

4. **List the cause of the concern:**

5. **Determine any necessary action(s) to correct the fault:**

6. Have your supervisor/instructor verify satisfactory completion of this procedure, any observations found, and any necessary action(s) recommended.

**Performance Rating**

CDX Tasksheet Number: C844

| 0 | 1 | 2 | 3 | 4 |
|---|---|---|---|---|
|   |   |   |   |   |

Supervisor/instructor signature _____ Date _____

© 2019 Jones & Bartlett Learning, LLC, an Ascend Learning Company

▶ **TASK** Diagnose oil leaks, emissions, and driveability concerns caused by the positive crankcase ventilation (PCV) system; determine needed action.

**MAST**
8E1

Time off_____

Time on_____

Total time_____

**CDX Tasksheet Number: C666**

**Vehicle used for this activity:**

Year _____ Make _____ Model_____

Odometer_____ VIN_____

1. **List the customer concern:**

2. **Research the particular concern in the appropriate service information.**

    a. **List the possible causes:**

    b. **List or print off and attach to this sheet the procedure for diagnosing the concern:**

3. **Using the recommended procedure, inspect the vehicle and diagnose any oil leaks, emissions, and driveability concerns caused by the PCV system. List your observations here:**

4. **List the cause of the concern:**

5. **Determine any necessary action(s) to correct the fault:**

6. Have your supervisor/instructor verify satisfactory completion of this procedure, any observations found, and any necessary action(s) recommended.

**Performance Rating**

CDX Tasksheet Number: C666

| | | | | |
|---|---|---|---|---|
| 0 | 1 | 2 | 3 | 4 |

Supervisor/instructor signature _____ Date _____

► **TASK** Inspect, test, service, and/or replace positive crankcase
ventilation (PCV) filter/breather, valve, tubes,
orifices, and hoses; perform needed action.

**MAST**
**8E2**

Time off_____

Time on_____

Total time_____

**CDX Tasksheet Number: C432**

1. **Research the PCV system on this vehicle in the appropriate service information.**

   a. **List the service interval for replacing the PCV valve:** _____ mi/km
   b. **List the service interval for replacing the breather filter:** _____ mi/km

2. **Follow the specified procedure to inspect and test the PCV system. List your observations for each component below:**

   a. **Filter/breather:**

   b. **PCV valve:**

   c. **Tubes, orifices, and hoses:**

3. **Determine any necessary action(s):**

4. **Have your supervisor/instructor verify your conclusions. Supervisor's/ instructor's initials:** _____

5. **Perform any necessary action(s) and list them here:**

© 2019 Jones & Bartlett Learning, LLC, an Ascend Learning Company

Fuel and Emissions Systems **39**

6. **Have your supervisor/instructor verify satisfactory completion of this procedure, any observations found, and any necessary action(s) recommended.**

**CDX Tasksheet Number: C432**

| 0 | 1 | 2 | 3 | 4 |
|---|---|---|---|---|
|   |   |   |   |   |

Supervisor/instructor signature _____ Date _____

© 2019 Jones & Bartlett Learning, LLC, an Ascend Learning Company

▶ **TASK** Diagnose the cause of excessive oil consumption, coolant consumption, unusual exhaust color, odor, and sound; determine needed action.

Time off_____

Time on_____

Total time_____

**CDX Tasksheet Number: C391**

**Vehicle used for this activity:**

Year _____ Make _____ Model_____

Odometer_____ VIN_____

1. **List the exhaust-related customer concern:**

2. **Research possible causes of the concern for this vehicle in the appropriate service information.**

   a. **List any possible causes:**

   b. **List any specified tests to pinpoint the problem:**

3. **With your supervisor's/instructor's permission, operate the vehicle to verify the concern. List your observations:**

4. **Follow the specified procedure to diagnose the concern. List your tests and results:**

5. **List the cause of the concern:**

6. Determine any necessary action(s) to correct the fault:




7. Have your supervisor/instructor verify satisfactory completion of this procedure, any observations found, and any necessary action(s) recommended.

**Performance Rating**

CDX Tasksheet Number: C391

| | | | | |
|---|---|---|---|---|
| 0 | 1 | 2 | 3 | 4 |

Supervisor/instructor signature _____ Date _____

▶ **TASK** Diagnose emissions and driveability concerns caused by the exhaust gas recirculation (EGR) system; inspect, test, service, and/or replace electrical/electronic sensors, controls, wiring, tubing, exhaust passages, vacuum/pressure controls, filters, and hoses of exhaust gas recirculation (EGR) systems; determine needed action.

**MAST**
**8E3**

Time off_____

Time on_____

Total time_____

**CDX Tasksheet Number: C667**

**Vehicle used for this activity:**

Year _____ Make _____ Model_____

Odometer_____ VIN_____

1. **List the EGR-related customer concern:**

2. **Research the particular concern in the appropriate service information.**

   a. **List the possible causes:**

   b. **List or print off and attach to this sheet the procedure for diagnosing the concern:**

3. **Using the recommended procedure, inspect and diagnose any emissions and driveability concerns caused by the EGR system. List your tests and observations here:**

4. **List the cause of the concern:**

5.  Determine any necessary action(s) to correct the fault:

6.  Research the procedure for inspecting and testing the electrical/electronic components of the EGR system on this vehicle in the appropriate service information.

    a.  List any EGR electrical specifications for this vehicle:

7.  Follow the specified procedure to inspect and test the EGR system components. List your observations for each component below:

    a.  EGR valve, if electrically operated:

    b.  EGR vacuum solenoid, if equipped:

    c.  EGR flow sensor, if equipped:

    d.  Electrical wiring:

8.  Determine any necessary action(s):

9.  Have your supervisor/instructor verify your conclusions. Supervisor's/instructor's initials: _____

10. Perform any necessary action(s) and list them here:

11. Research the procedure for inspecting and testing the EGR system on this vehicle in the appropriate service information.
    a. List the type of EGR valve this vehicle is equipped with: _____
    b. List the service interval for replacing any of the EGR system components:

12. Follow the specified procedure to inspect and test the EGR system. List your observations for each component below:
    a. EGR valve:

    b. EGR tubing and exhaust passages:

    c. Vacuum/pressure controls:

    d. Filters and hoses:

13. Determine any necessary action(s):

14. Have your supervisor/instructor verify your conclusions. Supervisor's/instructor's initials: _____

15. Perform any necessary action(s) and list them here:

16. Have your supervisor/instructor verify satisfactory completion of this procedure, any observations found, and any necessary action(s) recommended.

**Performance Rating**

CDX Tasksheet Number: C667

| 0 | 1 | 2 | 3 | 4 |
|---|---|---|---|---|
|   |   |   |   |   |

Supervisor/instructor signature _____ Date _____

Diagnose emissions and driveability concerns caused by the secondary air injection system; inspect, test, repair, and/or replace electrical/electronically-operated components and circuits of secondary air injection systems; determine needed action.

**MAST**
**8E4**

Time off_____

Time on_____

Total time_____

**CDX Tasksheet Number: C843**

**Vehicle used for this activity:**

Year _____ Make _____ Model _____

Odometer _____ VIN _____

1. **List the customer concern:**

2. **Research the particular concern in the appropriate service information.**

   a. **List the possible causes:**

3. **Using the recommended procedure, inspect and diagnose any emissions and driveability concerns caused by the secondary air injection and catalytic converter systems. List your tests and observations here:**

4. **Research the procedure for inspecting and testing the electrical/electronic components of the air injection system on this vehicle in the appropriate service information.**

   a. **List any air injection system electrical specifications for this vehicle:**

5. **Follow the specified procedure to inspect and test the air injection system components. List your observations for each component below:**

   a. **Air injection switching valve, if electrically operated:**

© 2019 Jones & Bartlett Learning, LLC, an Ascend Learning Company

   **b. Air injection bypass or diverter valve, if electrically operated:**

   **c. Air pump, if electrically operated:**

   **d. Electrical wiring:**

6. **Determine any necessary action(s):**

7. **Have your supervisor/instructor verify your conclusions. Supervisor's/instructor's initials: _____**

8. **Perform any necessary action(s) and list them here:**

9. **Have your supervisor/instructor verify satisfactory completion of this procedure, any observations found, and any necessary action(s) recommended.**

**Performance Rating**

**CDX Tasksheet Number: C843**

| 0 | 1 | 2 | 3 | 4 |
|---|---|---|---|---|

Supervisor/instructor signature _____ Date _____

▶ **TASK** Identify hybrid vehicle A/C system electrical circuits and the service/safety precautions.

**MAST**
7B4

Time off_____

Time on_____

Total time_____

**CDX Tasksheet Number: C827**

**Vehicle used for this activity:**

Year _____ Make _____ Model_____

Odometer_____ VIN_____

1. **Research the description and operation of a hybrid vehicle A/C system in the appropriate service information.**

    a. **What powers the A/C compressor (prime mover)?**

    b. **Does the manufacturer use a special designation for the A/C system electrical circuits? Yes: _____ No: _____**

       i. **If yes, what is it?**

    c. **List the voltage(s) that the A/C system electrical circuits operate on:**

    d. **How is the A/C compressor driven? V belt: _____ Serpentine belt: _____ Direct drive: _____ Other (specify below)**

       i. **Specified refrigerant: _____**

       ii. **Refrigerant capacity: _____ lb/kg**

       iii. **Specified lubricant: _____**

       iv. **Lubricant capacity: _____ oz/mL**

       v. **List the specified safety precautions when servicing this system:**

2. Have your supervisor/instructor verify satisfactory completion of this procedure, any observations found, and any necessary action(s) recommended.

**Performance Rating**

CDX Tasksheet Number: C827

| 0 | 1 | 2 | 3 | 4 |
|---|---|---|---|---|

Supervisor/instructor signature _____ Date _____

Identify safety precautions for high voltage systems on electric, hybrid, hybrid-electric, and diesel vehicles.

Time off_____

Time on_____

Total time_____

**CDX Tasksheet Number: C561**

1. **Research the safety precautions for all high-voltage systems and methods of identifying those systems on the electric, hybrid, hybrid-electric, or diesel vehicle.**

    a. **List the systems that use or create high voltage:**

    b. **List any safety precautions when working on or around these systems and circuits:**

2. **Locate and point out, on the vehicle, the high-voltage circuits and components to your instructor.**

3. **Have your supervisor/instructor verify satisfactory completion of this procedure, any observations found, and any necessary action(s) recommended.**

**Performance Rating**

**CDX Tasksheet Number: C561**

| 0 | 1 | 2 | 3 | 4 |

Supervisor/instructor signature _____ Date _____

Identify service precautions related to service of the
internal combustion engine of a hybrid vehicle.

**MAST**
**1A9**

Time off_____

Time on_____

Total time_____

**CDX Tasksheet Number: C900**

**Vehicle used for this activity:**

Year _____ Make _____ Model_____

Odometer_____ VIN_____

1. **Research the precautions when servicing an internal combustion engine on a hybrid vehicle in the appropriate service information. List all precautions:**

2. **Have your supervisor/instructor verify satisfactory completion of the procedure, any observations found, and any necessary action(s) recommended.**

**Performance Rating**

CDX Tasksheet Number: C900

| 0 | 1 | 2 | 3 | 4 |
|---|---|---|---|---|

Supervisor/instructor signature _____ Date _____

Identify hybrid vehicle auxiliary (12V) battery service,
repair, and test procedures.

**MAST**
6B9

Time off_____

Time on_____

Total time_____

**CDX Tasksheet Number: C874**

1. **Research the hybrid vehicle auxiliary (12V) battery service, repair, and test procedures in the appropriate service information.**

   a. **Does this vehicle use a 12V auxiliary battery? Yes: _____
   No: _____**

   b. **List any special testing, service, or repair procedures related to the 12V auxiliary battery:**

2. **If you performed any tests, services, or repairs on the 12V auxiliary battery, list all tests or service performed and any results:**

3. **Determine any necessary action(s):**

4. **Have your supervisor/instructor verify satisfactory completion of this procedure, any observations found, and any necessary action(s) recommended.**

**Performance Rating**

CDX Tasksheet Number: C874

| | | | | |
|---|---|---|---|---|
| 0 | 1 | 2 | 3 | 4 |

Supervisor/instructor signature _____ Date _____

▶ **TASK** Research vehicle service information including vehicle service history, service precautions, and technical service bulletins.

**MAST**
**8A2**

Time off_____

Time on_____

Total time_____

**CDX Tasksheet Number: C387**

1. **Using the VIN for identification, use the appropriate source to access the vehicle's service history in relation to prior related engine management work or customer concerns.**

    a. **List any related repairs/concerns, and their dates:**

2. **Using the VIN for identification, access any relevant technical service bulletins for the particular vehicle you are working on in relation to engine management updates or other service issues.**

    a. **List any related service bulletins (bulletin number and title):**

3. **Have your supervisor/instructor verify satisfactory completion of this procedure, any observations found, and any necessary action(s) recommended.**

**Performance Rating**

**CDX Tasksheet Number: C387**

| 0 | 1 | 2 | 3 | 4 |
|---|---|---|---|---|
|   |   |   |   |   |

Supervisor/instructor signature _____ Date _____

Demonstrate the use of the three Cs
(concern, cause, and correction).

Time off_____

Time on_____

Total time_____

**CDX Tasksheet Number: N/A**

1. Using the following scenario, write up the three Cs as listed on most repair orders. Assume that the customer authorized the recommended repairs.

   A vehicle has been brought to your shop with an engine performance/driveability concern. The customer tells you that the vehicle used to run rough only when accelerating up a hill but now it is running rough when accelerating even lightly. The MIL light also blinks when the engine is running rough. The customer thought it was bad gas, but after that tank ran out, the customer refilled it with good gas from a very reputable station and it still runs rough even after using half a tank. The customer authorizes your shop to perform a diagnosis and you find the following:

   a. P0305—Engine misfire on cylinder #5.
   b. #5 spark plug boot is leaking high voltage to the cylinder head under light load.
   c. All of the spark plugs are moderately worn.
   d. All of the spark plug wires are original. The vehicle is about 8 years old and has nearly 100,000 miles on it.
   e. Cylinder relative compression is within specifications.
   f. The air filter is dirty.
   g. The oil change is almost 1000 miles and 2 months overdue.
   h. The oil seals and gaskets look to be in good shape with no leaks.
   i. The water pump seal is starting to seep coolant and the coolant is a bit dirty.
   j. The belts look like they have been replaced recently.

   > **NOTE** Ask your instructor whether you should use a copy of the shop repair order or the three Cs below to record this information.

2. Concern/complaint:

3. Cause:

4. Correction:

5. **Other recommended service:**


6. **Have your supervisor/instructor verify satisfactory completion of this procedure, any observations found, and any necessary action(s) recommended.**

© 2019 Jones & Bartlett Learning, LLC, an Ascend Learning Company

**Performance Rating**

**CDX Tasksheet Number: N/A**

| 0 | 1 | 2 | 3 | 4 |
|---|---|---|---|---|

Supervisor/instructor signature _____ Date _____

Time off_____

Time on_____

Total time_____

**CDX Tasksheet Number: C386**

1. **List the customer concern:**

2. **Research the particular concern in the appropriate service information.**

   a. **List the possible causes:**

3. **Inspect the engine and management system to determine the cause of the concern.**

   a. **List the steps you took to determine the fault and the result for each step:**

4. **List the cause of the concern/complaint:**

5. **List the necessary action(s) to correct this fault:**

6. Have your supervisor/instructor verify satisfactory completion of this procedure, any observations found, and any necessary action(s) recommended.

**Performance Rating**

**CDX Tasksheet Number: C386**

| 0 | 1 | 2 | 3 | 4 |
|---|---|---|---|---|

Supervisor/instructor signature _____ Date _____

Time off_____

Time on_____

Total time_____

CDX Tasksheet Number: N/A

1. **Disable the ignition or fuel system so that the engine will crank, but not start.**

   NOTE Some vehicles can be put into "clear flood" mode by depressing the throttle to the floor before turning the ignition key to the "run" position. This prevents the fuel injectors from being activated. If your vehicle is equipped with this mode, hold the throttle down to the floor and try cranking the engine over (make sure you are prepared to turn off the ignition switch if the engine starts). You can also disable the engine by disconnecting the fuel injectors or ignition coils.

2. **Crank the engine over for approximately 5 seconds and listen to the cranking sound.**

   NOTE The engine should crank over at a normal speed. Too fast could mean low compression caused by bent valves or a slipped timing belt or chain. Too slow could mean a seized piston or bearing, or a faulty starting system. An uneven cranking sound may indicate grossly uneven compression pressures in the cylinders.

3. **List your observation(s):**

4. **Determine any necessary action(s):**

5. **Have your supervisor/instructor verify satisfactory completion of this procedure, any observations found, and any necessary action(s) recommended.**

**Performance Rating**

CDX Tasksheet Number: N/A

| | | | | |
|---|---|---|---|---|
| 0 | 1 | 2 | 3 | 4 |

Supervisor/instructor signature _____ Date _____

Perform engine absolute manifold pressure tests (vacuum/boost); determine needed action.

**CDX Tasksheet Number: C392**

1. **Find an appropriate vacuum hose to connect into.**

> **NOTE** Make sure the vacuum hose is connected to the intake manifold vacuum and you are not disconnecting anything that will affect the operation of the engine. If possible, the use of a vacuum tee will allow you to take the reading while allowing the vacuum to get to its intended device.

2. **Running Vacuum Test**

   a. **Describe the purpose of this test, the components or functions the test checks, and what the results might indicate:**

   b. **Start the engine, allow it to idle, and note the vacuum reading:**
   _____

   i. **Is the vacuum gauge needle relatively steady? Yes:** _____
   **No:** _____

   c. **Carefully raise the engine rpm to 2000 rpm and note the vacuum reading:** _____

   i. **Is the vacuum gauge needle relatively steady? Yes:** _____
   **No:** _____

   ii. **The vacuum reading should be higher at 2000 rpm than at idle. Is it?**
   **Yes:** _____ **No:** _____

   d. **Determine any necessary action(s):**

3. **Have your supervisor/instructor verify satisfactory completion of this procedure, any observations found, and any necessary action(s) recommended.**

**Performance Rating**

**CDX Tasksheet Number: C392**

| 0 | 1 | 2 | 3 | 4 |
|---|---|---|---|---|

Supervisor/instructor signature _____ Date _____

**MAST**
8A6

Time off_____

Time on_____

Total time_____

**CDX Tasksheet Number: C393**

1. Research the best option for disabling the cylinders on this vehicle in the appropriate service Information. The list that follows contains the most common methods. Choose the one that you plan on using.

   a. Disconnect individual spark plug wires or ignition coils. _____
   b. Disconnect individual fuel injectors (multi-port fuel injection only). _____
   c. Use a diagnostic scope to disable cylinders through the ignition primary circuit. _____
   d. Use a scan tool on vehicles with power balance capabilities. _____
   e. Use short sections of vacuum hose and a test light (option for waste spark ignition systems). _____

2. Determine from the service information if this vehicle has an idle control system. If it does, list how to best disable the system during this test:

3. Have your supervisor/instructor check the above answers. Supervisor's/instructor's initials: _____

4. If this vehicle is equipped with an idle control system, disable it and set the idle speed to an appropriate rpm.

   a. List the rpm here: _____

5. Disable the cylinders one at a time and record the rpm drop (not the rpm) of each cylinder.

   a. rpm drop: ---_____ ---_____ ---_____ ---_____ ---_____ ---_____ ---_____ ---_____

6. Determine any necessary action(s):

7. **Have your supervisor/instructor verify satisfactory completion of this procedure, any observations found, and any necessary action(s) recommended.**

**Performance Rating**

CDX Tasksheet Number: C393

| 0 | 1 | 2 | 3 | 4 |
|---|---|---|---|---|

Supervisor/instructor signature _____ Date _____

Perform cylinder cranking and running compression
tests; determine needed action.

Time off_____

Time on_____

Total time_____

**CDX Tasksheet Number: C709**

1. Research the procedure and specifications for performing both a cranking compression test and a running compression test on this vehicle in the appropriate service information.

2. List the conditions that must be met for the cranking compression test to be accurate (you may paraphrase):

3. Specifications

    a. Minimum compression pressure: _____ psi/kPa or %

    b. Maximum variation: _____ %

4. Cranking Compression Test: Perform the cranking compression test following the specified procedure. The top row in the table below is a standard test and the bottom row is a wet test using a small amount of clean engine oil. The wet test would normally be performed on engines that fail the standard test. List the readings obtained for each cylinder in the table.

| Cylinder | #1 | #2 | #3 | #4 | #5 | #6 | #7 | #8 |
|---|---|---|---|---|---|---|---|---|
| Standard test (psi/kPa) | | | | | | | | |
| Wet test(psi/kPa) | | | | | | | | |

    a. Calculate the difference between the highest and lowest cylinders (dry test): _____ %

5. Running Compression Test: Perform the running compression test following the specified procedure. List the readings obtained for each cylinder:

> **NOTE** Make sure the person snapping the throttle open is ready to turn off the ignition switch if the throttle sticks open.

| Cylinder | #1 | #2 | #3 | #4 | #5 | #6 | #7 | #8 |
|---|---|---|---|---|---|---|---|---|
| Idle (psi/kPa) | | | | | | | | |
| Snap throttle (psi/kPa) | | | | | | | | |

a. Determine any necessary action(s):

6. Have your supervisor/instructor verify satisfactory completion of this procedure, any observations found, and any necessary action(s) recommended.

© 2019 Jones & Bartlett Learning, LLC, an Ascend Learning Company

**Performance Rating**

CDX Tasksheet Number: C709

| 0 | 1 | 2 | 3 | 4 |
|---|---|---|---|---|

Supervisor/instructor signature _____ Date _____

Perform cylinder leakage tests; determine
needed action.

Time off_____

Time on_____

Total time_____

**CDX Tasksheet Number: C395**

1.  **List all of the possible places where compression can leak out of a cylinder:**

2.  **Remove the appropriate spark plugs to test the cylinder with the lowest compression pressure.**

3.  **Bring that piston up to top dead center on the compression stroke and install the cylinder leakage tester. List the reading you obtained.**

    a. **Cylinder #:** _____
    b. **Cylinder leakage:** _____ %
    c. **Leaking from:** _____

4.  **Perform this test on one other cylinder. List the reading you obtained. Before removing the cylinder leakage tester, call your supervisor/instructor over to verify the reading.**

    a. **Cylinder #:** _____
    b. **Cylinder leakage:** _____ %
    c. **Leaking from:** _____

5.  **Determine any necessary action(s):**

6.  **Have your supervisor/instructor verify satisfactory completion of this procedure, any observations found, and any necessary action(s) recommended.**

**Performance Rating**

CDX Tasksheet Number: C395

| 0 | 1 | 2 | 3 | 4 |
|---|---|---|---|---|

Supervisor/instructor signature _____ Date _____

**▶ TASK** Diagnose abnormal engine noises or vibration concerns; determine needed action.

**MAST 8A3**

Time off_____
Time on_____
Total time_____

**CDX Tasksheet Number: C390**

1. Ask your instructor to assign you a vehicle with an engine noise or vibration concern. List the customer concern:

2. Research possible causes of the concern for this vehicle in the appropriate service information.

   a. List any possible causes:

   b. List any specified tests to pinpoint the problem:

3. With your supervisor's/instructor's permission, operate the vehicle to verify the concern. List your observations:

4. Follow the service manual procedure to diagnose the concern. List your tests and results here:

5. Determine necessary action(s):

6. **Have your supervisor/instructor verify satisfactory completion of this procedure, any observations found, and any necessary action(s) recommended.**

**Performance Rating**

CDX Tasksheet Number: C390

| 0 | 1 | 2 | 3 | 4 |
|---|---|---|---|---|

Supervisor/instructor signature _____ Date _____

Inspect engine assembly for fuel, oil, coolant, and
other leaks; determine needed action.

**MAST**
1A4

**CDX Tasksheet Number: C004**

> **NOTE** If the vehicle's engine assembly is coated with leaking fluids and road dirt,
> you may need to pressure wash the engine before inspecting it for leaks. Some
> very small leaks, or leaks on engines that have a lot of accumulated residue, may
> be diagnosed with the use of a fluorescent dye and ultraviolet light. Check with
> your supervisor/instructor about which procedure to perform. Follow the dye check
> equipment manufacturer's instructions if you are performing this test.

> **NOTE** Fluid leaks can be hard to locate. Remember that gravity tends to pull any
> leaking fluid down. You will need to identify the highest point of the leak to locate
> its source. Fluids can also be flung from rotating parts, sprayed under pressure from
> pinhole leaks, or blown by airflow far from the source. Investigate carefully.

1. **Check for fluid leaks under the hood. List any leaks (component leaking and type
   of fluid):**

2. **Safely raise and secure the vehicle on a hoist.**

3. **Inspect the engine, cooling system, fuel system, transmission/transaxle, and any
   differentials for leaks. Identify the type of fluid leaking and the source of the leak
   for the following items:**

   a. **Engine:**

   b. **Fuel system:**

   c. **Cooling system:**

d. Transmission/transaxle:

e. Steering system:

f. Differentials:

4. Determine any necessary action(s):

5. Have your supervisor/instructor verify satisfactory completion of this procedure, any observations found, and any necessary action(s) recommended.

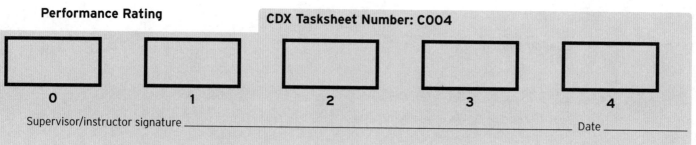

**Performance Rating**

CDX Tasksheet Number: C004

| 0 | 1 | 2 | 3 | 4 |

Supervisor/instructor signature _____ Date _____

**MAST**
**8A11**

**CDX Tasksheet Number: C400**

1. **Research the timing belt inspection procedure for this vehicle in the appropriate service information. List the following specifications:**

    a. **Timing belt replacement interval:** _____ **mi/km**

    b. **Is this engine equipped with variable valve timing (VVT)?**
       **Yes:** _____ **No:** _____

    c. **Draw a picture or print off a copy of the timing belt alignment diagram:**

2. **Following the specified procedure, verify correct camshaft timing. List your observations here:**

    a. **Is the camshaft timing correct? Yes:** _____ **No:** _____

3. **Have your supervisor/instructor verify satisfactory completion of this procedure, any observations found, and any necessary action(s) recommended.**

**Performance Rating**

**CDX Tasksheet Number: C400**

| | | | | |
|---|---|---|---|---|
| 0 | 1 | 2 | 3 | 4 |

Supervisor/instructor signature _____ Date _____

**MAST**
*8A10*

Time off_____

Time on_____

Total time_____

**CDX Tasksheet Number: C398**

1. Research the following specifications in the service information.

   a. Thermostat opening temperature: _____ °F/°C

   b. Temperature at which the electric fan comes on (if equipped): _____ °F/°C

   c. Temperature at which the fan clutch engages (on) (if equipped): _____ °F/°C

2. Apply the vehicle's parking brake and secure the vehicle with wheel chocks to prevent the vehicle from rolling.

3. Start the vehicle. Allow the vehicle to warm up while monitoring the engine temperature with the temp gun. Find the spot where the highest temperature reading is found on the engine side of the thermostat housing (on most engines). Monitor the temperature at that spot.

> **NOTE** The temperature should rise to between the thermostat opening temperature and the electric (or clutch) fan "on" temperature (if equipped). If this happens, continue to the next step. If the engine doesn't get that hot, diagnose the problem and go to step 4 below. Do NOT allow the engine to overheat!

   a. If the engine is equipped with an electric fan, the temperature should vary between the electric fan "on" temperature and the electric fan "off" temperature. Record these temperatures:

   i. Electric fan "on" temp: _____ °F/°C

   ii. Electric fan "off" temp: _____ °F/°C

   b. If the engine is equipped with a clutch fan, the temperature should rise above the thermostat opening temperature but not above the clutch fan engagement temperature. Record these two temperatures:

   i. Clutch fan "engaged" temp: _____ °F/°C

   ii. Clutch fan "disengaged" temp: _____ °F/°C

   c. If the engine is equipped with a mechanical fan without a clutch, the temperature should rise to, or slightly above, the thermostat opening temperature and should remain fairly steady. Record this operating temperature:

   i. Engine operating temperature: _____ °F/°C

4. If the engine did not reach the specified thermostat opening temperature, list the max temperature reached: _____ °F/°C

5. Determine any necessary action(s):

6. Have your supervisor/instructor verify satisfactory completion of this procedure, any observations found, and any necessary action(s) recommended.

**Performance Rating**

**CDX Tasksheet Number: C398**

| 0 | 1 | 2 | 3 | 4 |
|---|---|---|---|---|

Supervisor/instructor signature _____ Date _____

Access and use service information to perform step-by-step (troubleshooting) diagnosis.

**MAST**
**8B2**

**CDX Tasksheet Number: C841**

1. **The requirements for this task will be met by any number of Engine Performance diagnostic tasks you satisfactorily complete. Ask your instructor if a particular task you have completed, meets the criteria listed in the description of the task above. If so, list that task number and description:**

2. **List what service information you accessed and how you used it when performing the step-by-step diagnosis:**

3. **Have your supervisor/instructor verify your work. Supervisor's/instructor's initials _____**

**Performance Rating**

**CDX Tasksheet Number: C841**

| | | | | |
|---|---|---|---|---|
| 0 | 1 | 2 | 3 | 4 |

Supervisor/instructor signature _____ Date _____

Remove and replace spark plugs; inspect secondary
ignition components for wear and damage.

**MAST**
*8A4*

Time off_____

Time on_____

Total time_____

**CDX Tasksheet Number: C960**

1. Research the following specifications in the appropriate service information:
   a. Spark plug gap: _____ in/mm
   b. Ignition coil–primary winding resistance: _____ ohms
   c. Ignition coil–secondary winding resistance: _____ ohms
   d. Spark plug wire resistance: _____ ohms

2. Using the recommended equipment and following the correct procedure, inspect
   and test ignition primary and secondary windings of the ignition coil(s). List
   your observations here:
   a. Ignition coil–primary winding resistance: _____ ohms
   b. Ignition coil–secondary winding resistance: _____ ohms

3. Following the specified procedure, remove the spark plugs (keeping them in the
   same order) and inspect them. List your observations:

4. Following the specified procedure, inspect the secondary ignition wires. List your
   observations here:

5. Measure the resistance of each spark plug wire. List your measurements:

6. Have your supervisor/instructor verify removal of the plugs. Supervisor's/
   instructor's initials: _____

7. Following the specified procedure, gap the spark plugs, apply a small amount of
   antiseize to the threads if directed, reinstall them by hand, and torque them to
   the specified torque.

8. Have your supervisor/instructor verify satisfactory completion of this procedure, any observations found, and any necessary action(s) recommended.

**Performance Rating**

**CDX Tasksheet Number: C960**

| | | | | |
|---|---|---|---|---|
| 0 | 1 | 2 | 3 | 4 |

Supervisor/instructor signature _____ Date _____

► **TASK** Diagnose (troubleshoot) ignition system-related problems such as no-starting, hard starting, engine misfire, poor driveability, spark knock, power loss, poor mileage, and emissions concerns; determine needed action.

Time off_____

Time on_____

Total time_____

**CDX Tasksheet Number: C712**

**Vehicle used for this activity:**

Year _____ Make _____ Model_____

Odometer_____ VIN_____

1. **List the ignition system-related customer concern/complaint:**

2. **Verify the concern and list your observations here:**

3. **Research the particular concern in the appropriate service information and list the possible causes:**

4. **Using the specified equipment and the correct procedure, diagnose the concern. List your tests and results here:**

5. **What is causing the customer concern?**

6. **Determine any necessary action(s) to correct the fault(s):**

7. Have your supervisor/instructor verify satisfactory completion of this procedure, any observations found, and any necessary action(s) recommended.

**Performance Rating**

**CDX Tasksheet Number: C712**

| 0 | 1 | 2 | 3 | 4 |
|---|---|---|---|---|

Supervisor/instructor signature _____ Date _____

Inspect and test crankshaft and camshaft position sensor(s); determine needed action.

Time off_____

Time on_____

Total time_____

**CDX Tasksheet Number: C663**

**Vehicle used for this activity:**

Year _____ Make _____ Model_____

Odometer_____ VIN_____

1. List the crankshaft/camshaft sensor-related customer concern/complaint:

2. Research the particular concern in the appropriate service information and list the possible causes:

3. Using the specified equipment and the correct procedure, inspect and test the crankshaft and camshaft position sensor(s). List your test(s) and observations here:

4. What is causing the customer concern?

5. Determine any necessary action(s) to correct the fault(s):

6. Perform any necessary action(s) and note the results here:

7. Have your supervisor/instructor verify satisfactory completion of this procedure, any observations found, and any necessary action(s) recommended.

**Performance Rating**

CDX Tasksheet Number: C663

| 0 | 1 | 2 | 3 | 4 |
|---|---|---|---|---|

Supervisor/instructor signature _____ Date _____

**▶ TASK** Inspect, test, and/or replace ignition control module, powertrain/engine control module; reprogram/initialize as needed.

**MAST**
**8C3**

Time off_____

Time on_____

Total time_____

**CDX Tasksheet Number: C664**

**Vehicle used for this activity:**

Year _____ Make _____ Model_____

Odometer_____ VIN_____

1. **List the ignition control module/powertrain control module-related customer concern/complaint:**

2. **Research the particular concern in the appropriate service information and list the possible causes:**

3. **Using the specified equipment and the correct procedure, inspect, test, and/or replace the ignition control module or powertrain/engine control module. List your test(s) and observations here:**

4. **What is causing the customer concern?**

5. **Determine any necessary action(s) to correct the fault(s):**

6. **Perform any necessary action(s) and list the results here:**

7. Reprogram/initialize the module in accordance with the manufacturer's procedure if necessary. List your results:

8. Have your supervisor/instructor verify satisfactory completion of this procedure, any observations found, and any necessary action(s) recommended.

**Performance Rating**

**CDX Tasksheet Number: C664**

| 0 | 1 | 2 | 3 | 4 |
|---|---|---|---|---|

Supervisor/instructor signature _____ Date _____

Diagnose engine mechanical, electrical, electronic, fuel, and ignition concerns; determine needed action.

**MAST**
**8A9**

**CDX Tasksheet Number: C710**

1. **List the driveability-related customer concern:**

2. **Research the particular concern in the appropriate service information.**

   a. **List the possible causes:**

3. **Using the specified procedure, inspect and diagnose any engine mechanical, electrical, electronic, fuel, and ignition concerns. List your tests and results here:**

4. **List the cause of the concern:**

5. **Determine any necessary action(s) to correct the fault:**

6. **Have your supervisor/instructor verify satisfactory completion of this procedure, any observations found, and any necessary action(s) recommended.**

**Performance Rating**

**CDX Tasksheet Number: C710**

| 0 | 1 | 2 | 3 | 4 |
|---|---|---|---|---|

Supervisor/instructor signature _____ Date _____

**MAST**
**8B4**

Time off_____

Time on_____

Total time_____

**CDX Tasksheet Number: C661**

1. Research the following details in the appropriate service information:
   a. List which OBD monitors apply to this vehicle:

   b. List the parameters the "Catalyst" monitor must meet before showing a "Ready" status:

   c. List the parameters the "EVAP" monitor must meet before showing a "Ready" status:

2. Describe in your own words the importance of running all OBD monitors for repair verification:

3. Have your supervisor/instructor verify satisfactory completion of this procedure, any observations found, and any necessary action(s) recommended.

© 2019 Jones & Bartlett Learning, LLC, an Ascend Learning Company

**Performance Rating**

**CDX Tasksheet Number: C661**

| 0 | 1 | 2 | 3 | 4 |
|---|---|---|---|---|
|   |   |   |   |   |

Supervisor/instructor signature _____ Date _____

Retrieve and record diagnostic trouble codes (DTC), OBD monitor status, and freeze-frame data; clear codes when applicable.

**MAST**
**8B**

**CDX Tasksheet Number: C659**

1. **Connect the scan tool to the vehicle in accordance with the manufacturer's instructions; retrieve and record any diagnostic trouble codes:**

2. **List the monitor status for each OBD monitor:**

3. **List (or print off and attach) the freeze-frame data:**

4. **Clear codes when applicable. This may not necessarily be now.**

> **NOTE** Clearing the codes will also erase the OBD monitor status and freeze-frame data on most vehicles. Clear codes only when the service information directs you to do so.

5. **Have your supervisor/instructor verify satisfactory completion of this procedure, any observations found, and any necessary action(s) recommended.**

© 2019 Jones & Bartlett Learning, LLC, an Ascend Learning Company

**Performance Rating**

**CDX Tasksheet Number: C659**

| 0 | 1 | 2 | 3 | 4 |
|---|---|---|---|---|

Supervisor/instructor signature _____ Date _____

▶ TASK Inspect and test computerized engine control system sensors, powertrain/engine control module (PCM/ECM), actuators, and circuits using a graphing multimeter (GMM)/digital storage oscilloscope (DSO); perform needed action.

MAST
8B7

Time off_____

Time on_____

Total time_____

**CDX Tasksheet Number: C840**

1. **Research the following patterns/test procedures for this vehicle in the appropriate service information.**

   a. **Sketch (or print out) the specified oxygen sensor pattern (front):**

   b. **Sketch (or print out) the specified fuel injector pattern:**

2. **Connect the GMM or DSO to the oxygen sensor circuit, start the vehicle, allow the engine to warm up for the specified amount of time, and observe the pattern on the test equipment.**

   a. **Sketch or print off and attach to this sheet the pattern you obtained here:**

   b. **List your observation(s):**

3. **Connect the GMM or DSO to the fuel injector circuit, start the vehicle, allow the engine to warm up for the specified amount of time, and observe the pattern on the test equipment.**

   a. **Sketch or print off and attach to this sheet the pattern you obtained here:**

   b. **List your observation(s):**

4. Determine any necessary action(s):

5. Have your supervisor/instructor verify satisfactory completion of this procedure, any observations found, and any necessary action(s) recommended.

**Performance Rating**

CDX Tasksheet Number: C840

| 0 | 1 | 2 | 3 | 4 |

Supervisor/instructor signature _____ Date _____

▶ **TASK** Perform active tests of actuators using a scan tool; determine needed action.

**MAST**
**8B3**

Time off_____

Time on_____

Total time_____

**CDX Tasksheet Number: C867**

1. Connect the scan tool to the vehicle in accordance with the manufacturer's instructions and, while using the scan tool directions, perform active tests on at least two actuators. List the actuators tested and the results of those tests:

2. Determine any necessary action(s):

3. Have your supervisor/instructor verify satisfactory completion of this procedure, any observations found, and any necessary action(s) recommended.

**Performance Rating**

**CDX Tasksheet Number: C867**

| | | | | |
|---|---|---|---|---|
| 0 | 1 | 2 | 3 | 4 |

Supervisor/instructor signature _____ Date _____

Interpret diagnostic trouble codes (DTCs) and scan tool data related to the emissions control systems; determine needed action.

**MAST**
8E7

Time off_____

Time on_____

Total time_____

**CDX Tasksheet Number: C668**

**Vehicle used for this activity:**

Year _____ Make _____ Model_____

Odometer_____ VIN_____

1. **List the emissions system-related customer concern:**

2. **Research the particular concern in the appropriate service information.**

    a. **List the possible causes:**

3. **Using the correct equipment, retrieve and record diagnostic trouble codes, OBD monitor status, and freeze-frame data:**

    a. **List any stored DTCs and their descriptions:**

    b. **List the status of all monitors:**

    c. **List any freeze-frame data:**

4. **Using the data listed above, interpret the DTCs and scan tool data results. List your tests and results here:**

5. List the cause of the concern:

6. Determine any necessary action(s) to correct the fault:

7. Have your supervisor/instructor verify satisfactory completion of this procedure, any observations found, and any necessary action(s) recommended.

Diagnose the causes of emissions or driveability concerns with stored or active diagnostic trouble codes (DTC); obtain, graph, and interpret scan tool data.

**MAST**
**8B5**

Time off_____

Time on_____

Total time_____

**CDX Tasksheet Number: C660**

**Vehicle used for this activity:**

Year _____ Make _____ Model _____

Odometer _____ VIN _____

1. **List the emissions- or driveability-related customer concern:**

2. **Research the particular concern in the appropriate service information.**

    a. **List the possible causes:**

3. **Using the correct equipment, retrieve and record diagnostic trouble codes, OBD monitor status, and freeze-frame data, then interpret the scan tool data:**

    a. **List any stored DTCs and their descriptions:**

    b. **List the status of all monitors:**

    c. **List any freeze-frame data:**

4. **With the aid of the stored data or active diagnostic trouble codes, diagnose the cause of emissions or driveability concern. List your tests and results here:**

5. List the cause of the concern:

6. Determine any necessary action(s) to correct the fault:

7. Have your supervisor/instructor verify satisfactory completion of this procedure, any observations found, and any necessary action(s) recommended.

**Performance Rating**

**CDX Tasksheet Number: C660**

| 0 | 1 | 2 | 3 | 4 |
|---|---|---|---|---|

Supervisor/instructor signature _____ Date _____

Diagnose emissions or driveability concerns without stored
or active diagnostic trouble codes; determine needed action.

**MAST**
**8B6**

Time off_____

Time on_____

Total time_____

**CDX Tasksheet Number: C711**

**Vehicle used for this activity:**

Year _____ Make _____ Model_____

Odometer_____ VIN_____

1.  **List the emissions- or driveability-related customer concern:**

2.  **Research the particular concern in the appropriate service information.**

    a.  **List the possible causes:**

3.  **Follow the service manual procedure to diagnose the cause of the concern. List your tests and results here:**

4.  **List the cause of the concern:**

5.  **Determine any necessary action(s) to correct the fault:**

6. Have your supervisor/instructor verify satisfactory completion of this procedure, any observations found, and any necessary action(s) recommended.

**Performance Rating**

CDX Tasksheet Number: C711

| 0 | 1 | 2 | 3 | 4 |
|---|---|---|---|---|

Supervisor/instructor signature _____ Date _____

Diagnose driveability and emissions problems resulting from malfunctions of interrelated systems (cruise control, security alarms, suspension controls, traction controls, HVAC, automatic transmissions, non-OEM-installed accessories, or similar systems); determine needed action.

**MAST**
8B8

Time off_____

Time on_____

Total time_____

**CDX Tasksheet Number: C409**

**Vehicle used for this activity:**

Year _____ Make _____ Model _____

Odometer _____ VIN _____

1. **List the driveability- or emissions system-related customer concern (interrelated system problem):**

2. **Research the particular concern in the appropriate service information.**

   a. **List the possible causes:**

3. **Using the correct equipment, retrieve and record diagnostic trouble codes, OBD monitor status, and freeze-frame data:**

   a. **List any stored DTCs and their descriptions:**

   b. **List the status of all monitors:**

   c. **List any freeze-frame data:**

4. Using the data listed above, diagnose the cause of the customer concern. List your tests and results here:

5. List the cause of the concern:

6. Determine any necessary action(s) to correct the fault:

7. Have your supervisor/instructor verify satisfactory completion of this procedure, any observations found, and any necessary action(s) recommended.

**Performance Rating**

CDX Tasksheet Number: C409

| 0 | 1 | 2 | 3 | 4 |

Supervisor/instructor signature _____ Date _____

► **TASK** Use wiring diagrams during the diagnosis (troubleshooting) of electrical/electronic circuit problems.

**MAST**
**6A7**

Time off_____

Time on_____

Total time_____

**CDX Tasksheet Number: C952**

> **NOTE** This task requires diagnosis of an electrical problem. Please ask your instructor/supervisor to assign you a vehicle that qualifies for this task and several that follow.

1. List the customer concern/complaint:

2. Which electrical circuit(s) are involved?

3. How many circuit protection devices are there in this circuit? _____

   a. List the circuit protection devices in this circuit:

   b. List the circuit control devices in this circuit:

   c. Which side of the load(s) is controlled?

4. Diagnose the fault and list each test and its result:

5. Determine any necessary actions:

6. Have your supervisor/instructor verify satisfactory completion of this procedure, any observations found, and any necessary action(s) recommended.

**Performance Rating**

CDX Tasksheet Number: C952

| 0 | 1 | 2 | 3 | 4 |

Supervisor/instructor signature _____ Date _____

Inspect, test, repair, and/or replace components, connectors, terminals, harnesses, and wiring in electrical/electronic systems (including solder repairs); determine needed action.

**MAST**
**6A10**

Time off_____

Time on_____

Total time_____

**CDX Tasksheet Number: C299**

**Vehicle used for this activity:**

Year _____ Make _____ Model_____

Odometer_____ VIN_____

1. **Ask your instructor which of the items listed above you should inspect and test. List here:** _____

   **If needed locate the wiring diagram for the component that you are testing. Determine the purpose and operation of the suspected component. (Understanding how a component is designed to operate within a circuit will make it easier to diagnose.)**

2. **After inspection and testing of the item, list the needed repair:**

3. **Using the appropriate service information, determine the manufacturer's recommended procedure to complete the needed repair.**

4. **Have your instructor verify the repair procedure. Supervisor's/instructor's initials:** _____

5. **Carry out the suggested repair or replacement procedure. List your tests and results:**

6. **Determine any needed action(s):**

7. Have your supervisor/instructor verify satisfactory completion of this procedure, any observations found, and any needed action(s) recommended.

**Performance Rating**

CDX Tasksheet Number: C299

| 0 | 1 | 2 | 3 | 4 |
|---|---|---|---|---|
| □ | □ | □ | □ | □ |

Supervisor/instructor signature _____ Date _____

**MAST**
**6A12**

**CDX Tasksheet Number: C955**

1. Ask your instructor to assign a data bus wiring harness for you to perform this task on.

2. Research the proper steps to repair the data bus wiring harness in the appropriate service information.

   a. List the steps to properly repair the data bus wiring:

3. With your instructor's permission, cut one wire of the data bus system.

   a. Have your instructor verify the cut wire and repair procedure.
      Supervisor's/instructor's initials: _____

4. Perform the repair; be careful to follow all of the steps of the specified procedure.

5. What did you do to prevent electrical noise from affecting the repaired wires once they are back in service?

6. How did you insulate the soldered joint? _____

7. Have your supervisor/instructor verify satisfactory completion of this procedure, any observations found, and any necessary action(s) recommended.

**Performance Rating**

**CDX Tasksheet Number: C955**

| 0 | 1 | 2 | 3 | 4 |
|---|---|---|---|---|
|   |   |   |   |   |

Supervisor/instructor signature _____ Date _____

Demonstrate proper use of a digital multimeter
(DMM) when measuring source voltage, voltage drop
(including grounds), current flow, and resistance.

**MAST**
6A3

Time off_____

Time on_____

Total time_____

**CDX Tasksheet Number: C641**

> **NOTE** This task is best performed on either the CDX DVOM simulator, a physical simulator, or a bugged vehicle.

1. **Ask your instructor what lighting circuit he/she would like you to perform the following meter readings on. List circuit here:**

2. **Using the appropriate wiring diagram as a reference and a DMM, determine the following:**

   a. **Measured source voltage (at battery):** _____ **volts**
   b. **Measured voltage drop (positive side of circuit):** _____ **volts**
   c. **Measured voltage drop (negative side of circuit):** _____ **volts**
   d. **Measured resistance of light:** _____ **ohms**
   e. **Measured current flow through light:** _____ **amps**

3. **Were any of the readings out of specification? Yes: _____ No: _____**

   a. **List your observations:**

4. **Have your supervisor/instructor verify satisfactory completion of this procedure and any observations found.**

© 2019 Jones & Bartlett Learning, LLC, an Ascend Learning Company

**Performance Rating**

**CDX Tasksheet Number: C641**

| 0 | 1 | 2 | 3 | 4 |
|---|---|---|---|---|

Supervisor/instructor signature _____ Date _____

▶ TASK  Demonstrate proper use of a test light on an electrical circuit.

**MAST**
6A5

Time off_____

Time on_____

Total time_____

**CDX Tasksheet Number: C291**

1. **Test for proper operation of the test light by connecting it across the vehicle's battery terminals.**

   a. **Connect the clip end (negative) of the test light to the negative battery terminal.**

   b. **Touch the probe end of the test light to the positive battery terminal. The test light should light.**

   c. **Did the test light operate correctly? Yes: _____ No: _____**

> **NOTE** Please notify your supervisor/instructor if the test light did not operate correctly.

2. **Using the wiring diagram for the left tail lamp/parking light circuit of the assigned vehicle, identify the wire color for both the power (voltage) and ground (negative) wire.**

   i. **Power (positive): _____**

   ii. **Ground (negative): _____**

3. **Using the appropriate tools, remove the taillight assembly and disconnect the tail lamp connector. The headlamp switch should be set to "Off."**

   a. **Visually locate the power and ground wires, as described in step 2.**

   b. **Turn the headlamp switch to the "Park" position.**

   c. **Connect the clip end of the test light to an unpainted metal surface that is a good ground.**

   d. **Touch the test light probe to the positive wire of the vehicle harness tail lamp connector cavity.**

   i. **Did the test light come on? Yes: _____ No: _____**

   ii. **Please explain your results:**

   e. **With the test light probe still connected to the positive wire, test the ground wire by removing the clip end of the test light and touching it to the ground wire of the tail lamp connector cavity, being careful not to cause a short circuit by touching the clip to the probe. The light should come on if there is a good ground.**

   i. **Did the light come on? Yes: _____ No: _____**

3. **Based on your observations, determine any necessary action(s):**

4. Have your supervisor/instructor verify satisfactory completion of this procedure, any observations found, and any necessary action(s) recommended.

**Performance Rating**

CDX Tasksheet Number: C291

| 0 | 1 | 2 | 3 | 4 |
|---|---|---|---|---|

Supervisor/instructor signature _____ Date _____

▶ **TASK** Use fused jumper wires to check operation of electrical circuits.

**MAST**
6A6

**CDX Tasksheet Number: C295**

Time off_____

Time on_____

Total time_____

> **NOTE** Using a jumper wire to bypass components can cause damage if performed incorrectly. Never bypass the load in any circuit. Normally it is acceptable to bypass switches and some speed controlling resistors. If in doubt, ask your instructor.

1. **Ask your instructor to assign you a vehicle equipped with an electric cooling fan controlled by a relay.**

2. **Research the wiring diagram for the cooling fan circuit. Draw a diagram of that circuit.**

3. **Locate the cooling fan relay.**

4. **Draw a diagram of the relay socket and label each terminal with where the wire comes from, or goes to.**

5. **Label the diagram with the two points to which you believe the jumper wires should be placed.**

6. **Apply the parking brake and make sure the vehicle is in park or neutral.**

7. **Ask your instructor to verify your answers and where you plan to place the fused jumper wire. Have him/her watch you during the next portion of this task to ensure no damage is done to the vehicle's electrical system.**

   a. **Supervisor's/instructor's initials: _____**

8. **Turn the ignition switch to the run position, but do not start the vehicle (Key On, Engine Off - KOEO).**

9. **Use the fused jumper wire to activate the relay by jumping the terminals that connect to the relay contacts.**

   a. **List your observation(s):**

**10. Determine any necessary action(s):**

**11.** **Have your supervisor/instructor verify satisfactory completion of this procedure, any observations found, and any necessary action(s) recommended.**

**Performance Rating**

CDX Tasksheet Number: C295

| 0 | 1 | 2 | 3 | 4 |
|---|---|---|---|---|

Supervisor/instructor signature _____ Date _____

Inspect and test fusible links, circuit breakers, and fuses; determine needed action.

Time off_____

Time on_____

Total time_____

**CDX Tasksheet Number: C298**

1. **Using the appropriate service information, locate the fuse panel(s) for the vehicle/simulator you are assigned to.**

   a. **List the locations of the fuse panel(s) and circuit protection devices for this vehicle/simulator:**

2. **Use a test light to test each fuse and circuit breaker in one of the fuse boxes. List any circuit protection devices that are defective (open).**

> **NOTE** Circuit protection devices normally do not wear out. If a circuit protection device is found to be faulty, too much current was/is present. You should determine the reason for the fault.

3. **What is the rating (size) of the failed circuit protection device?**
   _____ **amps**

4. **Is the correct size fuse installed? Yes: _____ No: _____**

5. **Determine the cause for the circuit protection device to fail. List your tests and results below.**

6. **Determine any necessary action(s):**

7.  Have your supervisor/instructor verify satisfactory completion of this procedure, any observations found, and any necessary action(s) recommended.

**Performance Rating**

| 0 | 1 | 2 | 3 | 4 |
|---|---|---|---|---|

Supervisor/instructor signature _____ Date _____

**TASK** Inspect and test switches, connectors, and wires of
starter control circuits; determine needed action.

**MAST**
*6C5*

Time off_____

Time on_____

Total time_____

**CDX Tasksheet Number: C313**

1. Refering to the appropriate service information, draw a diagram of the starter
   control circuit (small wires) from battery positive terminal to the starter. On the
   diagram, list the components the current goes through to get to the starter.

   a. List the maximum specified voltage drop across the starter relay/solenoid
      contacts: _____ volts

2. Write a short description of how the starter control circuit operates to enable
   the starter to crank the engine:

3. Disable the vehicle's fuel or ignition system so it will not start.

4. Conduct the Starter Control Circuit Voltage Drop Test—Positive Side.

   a. List the voltmeter connection points in the circuit:

      DMM black lead: _____

      DMM red lead: _____

   b. Conduct the Starter Control Circuit Voltage Drop Test:

      What is the voltage drop on the positive side? _____ volts

      Is this reading within specifications? Yes: _____ No: _____

      i. If no, refer to the service information for further tests. List those tests
         and their results:

5. Determine any necessary action(s):

© 2019 Jones & Bartlett Learning, LLC, an Ascend Learning Company

Advanced Electrical/ Electronic Systems **123**

6. **Have your supervisor/instructor verify satisfactory completion of this procedure, any observations found, and any necessary action(s) recommended.**

**Performance Rating**

**CDX Tasksheet Number: C313**

| | | | | |
|---|---|---|---|---|
| 0 | 1 | 2 | 3 | 4 |

Supervisor/instructor signature _____ Date _____

Check electrical/electronic circuit waveforms; interpret readings and determine needed repairs.

**MAST**
.6A11

Time off_____

Time on_____

Total time_____

**CDX Tasksheet Number: C642**

**Vehicle used for this activity:**

Year _____ Make _____ Model_____

Odometer_____ VIN_____

1. **List the two most common types of electrical waveforms and describe how each of them differ:**

2. **Research various sensors for the vehicle you have been given.**

    a. **List at least two sensors that give an analog signal:**

    b. **List at least two sensors that give a digital signal:**

3. **Connect a lab scope to at least one analog sensor. Test the sensor, draw a diagram of the waveform, and list the name of the analog sensor:**

4. **Connect a lab scope to at least one digital sensor. Test the sensor, draw a diagram of the waveform, and list the name of the digital sensor:**

5. **Do these waveforms meet the manufacturer's specifications?**
    **Yes: _____ No: _____**

6. Determine any necessary action(s):

7. Have your supervisor/instructor verify satisfactory completion of this procedure, any observations found, and any necessary action(s) recommended.

**Performance Rating**

CDX Tasksheet Number: C642

| 0 | 1 | 2 | 3 | 4 |
|---|---|---|---|---|

Supervisor/instructor signature _____ Date _____

**MAST**
**8B4**

Time off_____

Time on_____

Total time_____

**CDX Tasksheet Number: C661**

1. **Research the following details in the appropriate service information:**
   a. **List which OBD monitors apply to this vehicle:**

   b. **List the parameters the "Catalyst" monitor must meet before showing a "Ready" status:**

   c. **List the parameters the "EVAP" monitor must meet before showing a "Ready" status:**

2. **Describe in your own words the importance of running all OBD monitors for repair verification:**

3. **Have your supervisor/instructor verify satisfactory completion of this procedure, any observations found, and any necessary action(s) recommended.**

**Performance Rating**

**CDX Tasksheet Number: C661**

| 0 | 1 | 2 | 3 | 4 |
|---|---|---|---|---|

Supervisor/instructor signature _____ Date _____

**MAST**
8B

**CDX Tasksheet Number: C659**

1. **Connect the scan tool to the vehicle in accordance with the manufacturer's instructions; retrieve and record any diagnostic trouble codes:**

2. **List the monitor status for each OBD monitor:**

3. **List (or print off and attach) the freeze-frame data:**

4. **Clear codes when applicable. This may not necessarily be now.**

> **NOTE** Clearing the codes will also erase the OBD monitor status and freeze-frame data on most vehicles. Clear codes only when the service information directs you to do so.

5. **Have your supervisor/instructor verify satisfactory completion of this procedure, any observations found, and any necessary action(s) recommended.**

**Performance Rating**

**CDX Tasksheet Number: C659**

| 0 | 1 | 2 | 3 | 4 |
|---|---|---|---|---|

Supervisor/instructor signature _____ Date _____

Inspect and test computerized engine control system sensors, powertrain/engine control module (PCM/ECM), actuators, and circuits using a graphing multimeter (GMM)/digital storage oscilloscope (DSO); perform needed action.

**MAST**
*8B7*

Time off_____

Time on_____

Total time_____

**CDX Tasksheet Number: C840**

1. **Research the following patterns/test procedures for this vehicle in the appropriate service information.**

    a. **Sketch (or print out) the specified oxygen sensor pattern (front):**

    b. **Sketch (or print out) the specified fuel injector pattern:**

2. **Connect the GMM or DSO to the oxygen sensor circuit, start the vehicle, allow the engine to warm up for the specified amount of time, and observe the pattern on the test equipment.**

    a. **Sketch or print off and attach to this sheet the pattern you obtained here:**

    b. **List your observation(s):**

3. **Connect the GMM or DSO to the fuel injector circuit, start the vehicle, allow the engine to warm up for the specified amount of time, and observe the pattern on the test equipment.**

    a. **Sketch or print off and attach to this sheet the pattern you obtained here:**

    b. **List your observation(s):**

4. Determine any necessary action(s):

5. Have your supervisor/instructor verify satisfactory completion of this procedure, any observations found, and any necessary action(s) recommended.

Perform active tests of actuators using a scan tool; determine needed action.

Time off_____

Time on_____

Total time_____

**CDX Tasksheet Number: C867**

1. Connect the scan tool to the vehicle in accordance with the manufacturer's instructions and, while using the scan tool directions, perform active tests on at least two actuators. List the actuators tested and the results of those tests:

2. Determine any necessary action(s):

3. Have your supervisor/instructor verify satisfactory completion of this procedure, any observations found, and any necessary action(s) recommended.

© 2019 Jones & Bartlett Learning, LLC, an Ascend Learning Company

**Performance Rating**

**CDX Tasksheet Number: C867**

| 0 | 1 | 2 | 3 | 4 |
|---|---|---|---|---|

Supervisor/instructor signature _____ Date _____

▶ **TASK** | Interpret diagnostic trouble codes (DTCs) and scan tool data related to the emissions control systems; determine needed action.

**MAST**
**8E7**

**CDX Tasksheet Number: C668**

**Vehicle used for this activity:**

Year _____ Make _____ Model _____

Odometer _____ VIN _____

1. **List the emissions system-related customer concern:**

2. **Research the particular concern in the appropriate service information.**

    a. **List the possible causes:**

3. **Using the correct equipment, retrieve and record diagnostic trouble codes, OBD monitor status, and freeze-frame data:**

    a. **List any stored DTCs and their descriptions:**

    b. **List the status of all monitors:**

    c. **List any freeze-frame data:**

4. **Using the data listed above, interpret the DTCs and scan tool data results. List your tests and results here:**

5. List the cause of the concern:

6. Determine any necessary action(s) to correct the fault:

7. Have your supervisor/instructor verify satisfactory completion of this procedure, any observations found, and any necessary action(s) recommended.

**Performance Rating**

CDX Tasksheet Number: C668

| 0 | 1 | 2 | 3 | 4 |
|---|---|---|---|---|

Supervisor/instructor signature _____ Date _____

**▶ TASK** Diagnose the causes of emissions or driveability concerns with stored or active diagnostic trouble codes (DTC); obtain, graph, and interpret scan tool data.

**MAST**
**8B5**

Time off_____

Time on_____

Total time_____

**CDX Tasksheet Number: C660**

**Vehicle used for this activity:**

Year _____ Make _____ Model_____

Odometer_____ VIN_____

1. **List the emissions- or driveability-related customer concern:**

2. **Research the particular concern in the appropriate service information.**

   a. **List the possible causes:**

3. **Using the correct equipment, retrieve and record diagnostic trouble codes, OBD monitor status, and freeze-frame data, then interpret the scan tool data:**

   a. **List any stored DTCs and their descriptions:**

   b. **List the status of all monitors:**

   c. **List any freeze-frame data:**

4. **With the aid of the stored data or active diagnostic trouble codes, diagnose the cause of emissions or driveability concern. List your tests and results here:**

5. List the cause of the concern:

6. Determine any necessary action(s) to correct the fault:

7. Have your supervisor/instructor verify satisfactory completion of this procedure, any observations found, and any necessary action(s) recommended.

**Performance Rating**

CDX Tasksheet Number: C660

| 0 | 1 | 2 | 3 | 4 |
|---|---|---|---|---|

Supervisor/instructor signature _____ Date _____

Diagnose emissions or driveability concerns without stored or active diagnostic trouble codes; determine needed action.

**MAST**
**8B6**

Time off_____

Time on_____

Total time_____

**CDX Tasksheet Number: C711**

**Vehicle used for this activity:**

Year _____ Make _____ Model_____

Odometer_____ VIN_____

1. **List the emissions- or driveability-related customer concern:**

2. **Research the particular concern in the appropriate service information.**

   a. **List the possible causes:**

3. **Follow the service manual procedure to diagnose the cause of the concern. List your tests and results here:**

4. **List the cause of the concern:**

5. **Determine any necessary action(s) to correct the fault:**

6. Have your supervisor/instructor verify satisfactory completion of this procedure, any observations found, and any necessary action(s) recommended.

**Performance Rating**

**CDX Tasksheet Number: C711**

| | | | | |
|---|---|---|---|---|
| 0 | 1 | 2 | 3 | 4 |

Supervisor/instructor signature _____ Date _____

Diagnose driveability and emissions problems resulting from malfunctions of interrelated systems (cruise control, security alarms, suspension controls, traction controls, HVAC, automatic transmissions, non-OEM-installed accessories, or similar systems); determine needed action.

**MAST**
**8B8**

Time off_____

Time on_____

Total time_____

**CDX Tasksheet Number: C409**

**Vehicle used for this activity:**

Year _____ Make _____ Model _____

Odometer _____ VIN _____

1. **List the driveability- or emissions system-related customer concern (interrelated system problem):**

2. **Research the particular concern in the appropriate service information.**

   a. **List the possible causes:**

3. **Using the correct equipment, retrieve and record diagnostic trouble codes, OBD monitor status, and freeze-frame data:**

   a. **List any stored DTCs and their descriptions:**

   b. **List the status of all monitors:**

   c. **List any freeze-frame data:**

4. Using the data listed above, diagnose the cause of the customer concern. List your tests and results here:

5. List the cause of the concern:

6. Determine any necessary action(s) to correct the fault:

7. Have your supervisor/instructor verify satisfactory completion of this procedure, any observations found, and any necessary action(s) recommended.

**Performance Rating**

**CDX Tasksheet Number: C409**

| | | | | |
|---|---|---|---|---|
| 0 | 1 | 2 | 3 | 4 |

Supervisor/instructor signature _____ Date _____

Diagnose body electronic system circuits using a scan tool; check for module communication errors (data communication bus systems); determine needed action.

**MAST**
**6G5**

**CDX Tasksheet Number: C338**

1. Locate "diagnosis of body electronic systems with a scan tool" in the appropriate service information for the vehicle you are working on.

   a. List the safety precautions to be taken when working on the body electronic systems:

   b. List the diagnostic procedures for the body electronic systems (or print and attach copy):

2. Check for any DTCs (diagnostic trouble codes) in the BCM (body control module) and list them and their descriptions here:

3. Following the specified procedure, diagnose faults in the body electronic system. List your tests and observations:

4. Determine any needed action(s) to correct the fault:

5. Have your supervisor/instructor verify satisfactory completion of this procedure, any observations found, and any needed action(s) recommended.

**Performance Rating**

**CDX Tasksheet Number: C338**

|  |  |  |  |  |
|---|---|---|---|---|
| 0 | 1 | 2 | 3 | 4 |

Supervisor/instructor signature _____ Date _____

▶ **TASK** Describe the process for software transfers, software updates, or reprogramming of electronic modules.

**MAST**
6G6

Time off_____

Time on_____

Total time_____

**CDX Tasksheet Number: C649**

**Vehicle used for this activity:**

Year _____ Make _____ Model_____

Odometer_____ VIN_____

1. **List the customer concern(s) related to software updates or the need for reprogramming electronic modules:**

2. **Verify the concern and list your observations including any codes, their descriptions, or any TSBs:**

3. **Research the correct method to perform software transfers, software updates, or reprogramming on electronic modules in appropriate service information.**

   a. **List any precautions here:**

   b. **List the steps needed to reprogram the electronic module (or print and attach):**

   c. **Have your instructor verify your process:** _____

4. Have your supervisor/instructor verify satisfactory completion of this procedure, any observations found, and any necessary action(s) recommended.

**Performance Rating**

CDX Tasksheet Number: C649

| | | | | |
|---|---|---|---|---|
| 0 | 1 | 2 | 3 | 4 |

Supervisor/instructor signature _____ Date _____

▶ TASK Diagnose operation of safety systems and related circuits (such as: horn, airbags, seat belt pretensioners, occupancy classification, wipers, washers, speed control/collision avoidance, heads-up display, park assist, and back-up camera); determine needed repairs.

**MAST**
**6G4**

Time off_____

Time on_____

Total time_____

**CDX Tasksheet Number: C327**

1. **Ask your instructor to assign a vehicle/simulator with a fault in a safety system. List the system:**

2. **List the customer concern/complaint:**

3. **Locate the diagnosis section and the wiring diagram for the safety system fault in the appropriate service information for the vehicle you are working on. Briefly describe the diagnostic procedure for this vehicle's safety system (or attach diagnosis printout):**

4. **Following the specified procedure, diagnose faults in the safety system. List your tests and their results:**

5. **List the cause of the customer concern/complaint:**

6. **Determine any needed repair(s) to correct the fault:**

7. Have your supervisor/instructor verify satisfactory completion of this procedure, any observations found, and any needed repair(s) recommended.

**Performance Rating**

CDX Tasksheet Number: C327

| 0 | 1 | 2 | 3 | 4 |
|---|---|---|---|---|

Supervisor/instructor signature _____ Date _____

Diagnose operation of security/anti-theft systems and related circuits (such as: theft deterrent, door locks, remote keyless entry, remote start, and starter/fuel disable); determine needed repairs.

**MAST**
**6G2**

Time off_____

Time on_____

Total time_____

**CDX Tasksheet Number: C340**

**Vehicle used for this activity:**

Year _____ Make _____ Model_____

Odometer_____ VIN_____

1. **Locate the diagnostic procedure for the security/anti-theft system in the appropriate service information for the vehicle you are working on.**

    a. **List the safety precautions to be taken when working on the security/anti-theft system:**

    b. **List the diagnostic procedures for the security/anti-theft system (or print and attach copy):**

2. **Check for any DTCs in the security/anti-theft system. List the DTCs and their descriptions here:**

3. **Following the specified procedure, diagnose faults in the security/anti-theft system. List your tests and observations:**

4. **Determine any needed repair(s) to correct the fault:**

5. Have your supervisor/instructor verify satisfactory completion of this procedure, any observations found, and any needed repair(s) recommended.

**Performance Rating**

CDX Tasksheet Number: C340

| | | | | |
|---|---|---|---|---|
| 0 | 1 | 2 | 3 | 4 |

Supervisor/instructor signature _____ Date _____

Diagnose operation of comfort and convenience accessories and related circuits (such as: power window, power seats, pedal height, power locks, trunk locks, remote start, moon roof, sun roof, sun shade, remote keyless entry, voice activation, steering wheel controls, back-up camera, park assist, cruise control, and auto dimming headlamps); determine needed repairs.

**MAST**
*6G1*

Time off_____

Time on_____

Total time_____

**CDX Tasksheet Number: C330**

1. **Ask your instructor to assign a vehicle with a fault in a comfort and convenience accessory circuit. List the circuit:**

2. **List the customer concern/complaint:**

3. **Locate the diagnosis section and the wiring diagram for the comfort and convenience accessory fault in the appropriate service information for the vehicle you are working on. Briefly describe the diagnostic procedure for this vehicle's comfort and convenience accessory circuit (or attach diagnosis printout):**

4. **Following the specified procedure, diagnose faults in the comfort and convenience accessory circuit. List your tests and their results:**

5. **List the cause of the customer concern/complaint:**

6. **Determine any needed repair(s) to correct the fault:**

7. Have your supervisor/instructor verify satisfactory completion of this procedure, any observations found, and any needed repair(s) recommended.

**Performance Rating**

CDX Tasksheet Number: C330

| | | | | |
|---|---|---|---|---|
| 0 | 1 | 2 | 3 | 4 |

Supervisor/instructor signature _____ Date _____

**MAST**
**8A2**

**CDX Tasksheet Number: C387**

1. **Using the VIN for identification, use the appropriate source to access the vehicle's service history in relation to prior related engine management work or customer concerns.**

   a. **List any related repairs/concerns, and their dates:**

2. **Using the VIN for identification, access any relevant technical service bulletins for the particular vehicle you are working on in relation to engine management updates or other service issues.**

   a. **List any related service bulletins (bulletin number and title):**

3. **Have your supervisor/instructor verify satisfactory completion of this procedure, any observations found, and any necessary action(s) recommended.**

**Performance Rating**

**CDX Tasksheet Number: C387**

| 0 | 1 | 2 | 3 | 4 |
|---|---|---|---|---|

Supervisor/instructor signature _____ Date _____

**MAST**
**8B2**

Time off_____

Time on_____

Total time_____

**CDX Tasksheet Number: C841**

1. The requirements for this task will be met by any number of Engine Performance diagnostic tasks you satisfactorily complete. Ask your instructor if a particular task you have completed, meets the criteria listed in the description of the task above. If so, list that task number and description:

2. List what service information you accessed and how you used it when performing the step-by-step diagnosis:

3. Have your supervisor/instructor verify your work. Supervisor's/instructor's initials _____

**Performance Rating**

**CDX Tasksheet Number: C841**

| 0 | 1 | 2 | 3 | 4 |
|---|---|---|---|---|

Supervisor/instructor signature _____ Date _____

► **TASK** Remove and replace spark plugs; inspect secondary ignition components for wear and damage.

**MAST**
8A4

Time off_____

Time on_____

Total time_____

**CDX Tasksheet Number: C960**

1. Research the following specifications in the appropriate service information:

   a. Spark plug gap: _____ in/mm
   b. Ignition coil–primary winding resistance: _____ ohms
   c. Ignition coil–secondary winding resistance: _____ ohms
   d. Spark plug wire resistance: _____ ohms

2. Using the recommended equipment and following the correct procedure, inspect and test ignition primary and secondary windings of the ignition coil(s). List your observations here:

   a. Ignition coil–primary winding resistance: _____ ohms
   b. Ignition coil–secondary winding resistance: _____ ohms

3. Following the specified procedure, remove the spark plugs (keeping them in the same order) and inspect them. List your observations:

4. Following the specified procedure, inspect the secondary ignition wires. List your observations here:

5. Measure the resistance of each spark plug wire. List your measurements:

6. Have your supervisor/instructor verify removal of the plugs. Supervisor's/instructor's initials: _____

7. Following the specified procedure, gap the spark plugs, apply a small amount of antiseize to the threads if directed, reinstall them by hand, and torque them to the specified torque.

8. **Have your supervisor/instructor verify satisfactory completion of this procedure, any observations found, and any necessary action(s) recommended.**

**Performance Rating**

CDX Tasksheet Number: C960

| 0 | 1 | 2 | 3 | 4 |
|---|---|---|---|---|

Supervisor/instructor signature _____ Date _____

▶ **TASK** Identify and interpret engine performance concerns; determine needed action.

**MAST**
**8A1**

**CDX Tasksheet Number: C386**

1. List the customer concern:

2. Research the particular concern in the appropriate service information.

   a. List the possible causes:

3. Inspect the engine and management system to determine the cause of the concern.

   a. List the steps you took to determine the fault and the result for each step:

4. List the cause of the concern/complaint:

5. List the necessary action(s) to correct this fault:

6. Have your supervisor/instructor verify satisfactory completion of this procedure, any observations found, and any necessary action(s) recommended.

**Performance Rating**

CDX Tasksheet Number: C386

| | | | | |
|---|---|---|---|---|
| 0 | 1 | 2 | 3 | 4 |

Supervisor/instructor signature _____ Date _____

▶ **TASK** Diagnose (troubleshoot) ignition system-related problems such as no-starting, hard starting, engine misfire, poor driveability, spark knock, power loss, poor mileage, and emissions concerns; determine needed action.

**MAST**
**8C1**

Time off_____

Time on_____

Total time_____

**CDX Tasksheet Number: C712**

**Vehicle used for this activity:**

Year _____ Make _____ Model_____

Odometer_____ VIN_____

1. **List the ignition system-related customer concern/complaint:**

2. **Verify the concern and list your observations here:**

3. **Research the particular concern in the appropriate service information and list the possible causes:**

4. **Using the specified equipment and the correct procedure, diagnose the concern. List your tests and results here:**

5. **What is causing the customer concern?**

6. **Determine any necessary action(s) to correct the fault(s):**

© 2019 Jones & Bartlett Learning, LLC, an Ascend Learning Company

7. Have your supervisor/instructor verify satisfactory completion of this procedure, any observations found, and any necessary action(s) recommended.

**Performance Rating**

CDX Tasksheet Number: C712

| 0 | 1 | 2 | 3 | 4 |
|---|---|---|---|---|

Supervisor/instructor signature _____ Date _____

Time off_____

Time on_____

Total time_____

**CDX Tasksheet Number: C663**

**Vehicle used for this activity:**

Year _____ Make _____ Model_____

Odometer_____ VIN_____

1. **List the crankshaft/camshaft sensor-related customer concern/complaint:**

2. **Research the particular concern in the appropriate service information and list the possible causes:**

3. **Using the specified equipment and the correct procedure, inspect and test the crankshaft and camshaft position sensor(s). List your test(s) and observations here:**

4. **What is causing the customer concern?**

5. **Determine any necessary action(s) to correct the fault(s):**

6. **Perform any necessary action(s) and note the results here:**

7. Have your supervisor/instructor verify satisfactory completion of this procedure, any observations found, and any necessary action(s) recommended.

**Performance Rating**

CDX Tasksheet Number: C663

| | | | | |
|---|---|---|---|---|
| 0 | 1 | 2 | 3 | 4 |

Supervisor/instructor signature _____ Date _____

Inspect, test, and/or replace ignition control module, powertrain/engine control module; reprogram/initialize as needed.

Time off_____

Time on_____

Total time_____

**CDX Tasksheet Number: C664**

**Vehicle used for this activity:**

Year _____ Make _____ Model_____

Odometer_____ VIN_____

1. **List the ignition control module/powertrain control module-related customer concern/complaint:**

2. **Research the particular concern in the appropriate service information and list the possible causes:**

3. **Using the specified equipment and the correct procedure, inspect, test, and/or replace the ignition control module or powertrain/engine control module. List your test(s) and observations here:**

4. **What is causing the customer concern?**

5. **Determine any necessary action(s) to correct the fault(s):**

6. **Perform any necessary action(s) and list the results here:**

7. **Reprogram/initialize the module in accordance with the manufacturer's procedure if necessary. List your results:**

8. **Have your supervisor/instructor verify satisfactory completion of this procedure, any observations found, and any necessary action(s) recommended.**

**Performance Rating**

**CDX Tasksheet Number: C664**

| | | | | |
|---|---|---|---|---|
| 0 | 1 | 2 | 3 | 4 |

Supervisor/instructor signature _____ Date _____

Perform slow/fast battery charge according to manufacturer's recommendations.

Time off_____

Time on_____

Total time_____

**CDX Tasksheet Number: C819**

> **NOTE** Recharging a battery differs from manufacturer to manufacturer. It is important that you follow the recharging steps recommended by the manufacturer of the battery that is assigned to you.

1. Research slow and/or fast battery charging for this vehicle battery in the appropriate service information. Follow all directions. If no directions are given, use the following information:

   It is best to disconnect the negative battery terminal when charging a battery. Consider using a memory minder to maintain the memories on electronic control modules.

   The ideal rate for charging a battery can be found by dividing the battery's CCA by 70.

   To find the maximum charging rate for fast charging a battery, divide the battery's CCA by 40.

   The faster a battery is charged, the shorter its life.

   Do not exceed: 15.5V on a flooded cell battery; 14.8V on an AGM battery; or 14.3V on a gel cell battery.

2. List the steps for recharging this battery:

3. What method is recommended for recharging the battery?
   Slow charge: _____ Fast charge: _____

   a. Have your supervisor/instructor verify the steps above. Supervisor's/instructor's initials: _____

4. Charge the battery according to the manufacturer's recommendations.

   a. How long did the battery charge? _____ time
   b. What was the highest amperage reading during charging? _____ amps
   c. What was the lowest amperage reading during charging? _____ amps
   d. What was the highest voltage during charging? _____ volts
   e. How did you determine the battery was fully charged?

5. Determine any necessary action(s):

6. Have your supervisor/instructor verify satisfactory completion of this procedure, any observations found, and any necessary action(s) recommended.

**Performance Rating**

CDX Tasksheet Number: C819

| 0 | 1 | 2 | 3 | 4 |
|---|---|---|---|---|

Supervisor/instructor signature _____ Date _____

**MAST**
**6B6**

Time off_____

Time on_____

Total time_____

**CDX Tasksheet Number: C820**

1. Research "starting a vehicle with a dead battery" or "jump starting procedures" in the appropriate service information for the vehicle you are working on. List the steps as outlined in the service information.

> **NOTE** Caution: Some vehicle manufacturers prohibit jump-starting of their vehicles. If this is the case, inform your supervisor/instructor.

> **NOTE** Follow these steps exactly!

2. Why is the last connection away from the battery, preferably on an unpainted solid metal component connected to the engine block?

3. Have your supervisor/instructor verify your answers. Supervisor's/instructor's initials: _____

4. Connect the jumper cables as outlined in the service information or connect the auxiliary power supply (jump box) as was outlined in the service information.

5. Start the engine.

6. Remove the cables in the reverse order as they were installed.

7. Have your supervisor/instructor verify satisfactory completion of this procedure, any observations found, and any necessary action(s) recommended.

**Performance Rating**

**CDX Tasksheet Number: C820**

| | | | | |
|---|---|---|---|---|
| 0 | 1 | 2 | 3 | 4 |

Supervisor/instructor signature _____ Date _____

Inspect and clean battery; fill battery cells; check battery cables, connectors, clamps, and hold-downs.

Time off_____

Time on_____

Total time_____

**CDX Tasksheet Number: C644**

1. On the vehicle that was assigned to you by your supervisor/instructor, and following all steps listed in the service information, disconnect the negative battery terminal and move it out of the way so it cannot touch the terminal, or spring back against it. (Consider using a memory minder.)

2. Disconnect the positive battery terminal and move it out of the way. Place a glove or other insulating material over the end of the battery cable to prevent shorting out the memory minder.

3. Remove the battery hold-down so that the battery is sitting in the battery tray or box.

4. Remove the battery from the battery tray.

5. Inspect the battery hold-down hardware and the battery tray. List your observations:

6. Clean the battery, battery terminals, battery tray, and hold-down hardware with a suitable cleaner or by mixing baking soda and water.

   NOTE The consistency of the baking soda and water should be like a thin paste. The use of a small brush will help the cleaning process.

7. Rinse the components with lots of clean water. Wipe the components dry with some paper towels.

   NOTE DO NOT USE COMPRESSED AIR! It can blow acid around.

8. Clean the battery terminals and posts with a battery terminal cleaner.

9. Check the battery electrolyte level. This can be done only on non-maintenance-free batteries. If the level is low, add only distilled water to the proper level.

   a. Have your supervisor/instructor check your work. Supervisor's/instructor's initials: _____

10. Install the battery and hold-down hardware, and reconnect the cables as outlined in the service information.

11. Install a battery terminal protective spray onto the battery terminals.

12. Determine any necessary action(s):

13. **Have your supervisor/instructor verify satisfactory completion of this procedure, any observations found, and any necessary action(s) recommended.**

**MAST**
*6B1*

Time off_____

Time on_____

Total time_____

**CDX Tasksheet Number: C302**

1.  **Research the following specifications for this vehicle in the appropriate service information.**

     a.  **Specified battery capacity: _____ cold cranking amps (CCA)**
     b.  **Group size, if specified: _____ BCI group**

> **NOTE** Check with your supervisor/instructor which of the following tests you are to perform, or whether you should perform all of them.

2.  **Perform a Specific Gravity Test. The battery must have removable vent caps.**

     a.  **Locate and review the "Specific Gravity State of Charge Test" in the appropriate service information.**
     b.  **Clean the top of the battery.**

> **NOTE** This must be done prior to the removal of the vent caps.

     c.  **Remove the vent caps.**
     d.  **Verify that the electrolyte level is high enough above the cells to fill the hydrometer.**
     e.  **Draw enough electrolyte from a cell so the float is suspended. Determine the specific gravity reading and return the electrolyte into the cell. Repeat this for each cell and record your readings below. Be sure to compensate for temperature if you are using a hydrometer that is not automatically temperature compensated.**

     **Cell #1: _____**
     **Cell #2: _____**
     **Cell #3: _____**
     **Cell #4: _____**
     **Cell #5: _____**
     **Cell #6: _____**

     f.  **Calculate the maximum difference between the cell readings: _____**
     g.  **What is the maximum allowable difference in cell readings: _____**
     h.  **Compare the readings to the information in the service information, and list the state of charge: _____ %**
     i.  **Clean the hydrometer and tools.**

3.  **Perform an Open Circuit Voltage Test. This test is for maintenance-free or non-vented batteries.**

     a.  **Locate and review the "Open Circuit Voltage Test" in the service Information.**
     b.  **Make sure the engine is off and the battery is stabilized. If the battery has just been recharged, you must remove the surface charge. Wait at least 5 minutes after removing the surface charge before measuring the open circuit voltage. Please follow the manufacturer's recommendations closely.**

c. Prepare the digital multimeter (DMM) to measure voltage.

d. Place the red lead on the positive post/terminal and the black lead on the negative post/terminal.

e. What is the measured voltage (open-circuit voltage) of the battery? _____ volts

f. The table below represents the open-circuit voltage of the battery. Please select the battery's percent of charge as it relates to the voltage measured.

| Voltage | Percent Charge |
|---|---|
| 12.6 or greater | 100 |
| 12.4–12.6 | 75–100 |
| 12.2–12.4 | 50–75 |
| 12.0–12.2 | 25–50 |
| 11.7–12.0 | 0–25 |
| 0.0–11.7 | 0; no charge |

4. Perform a Conductance Test.

a. Review the process for performing a battery conductance test.

b. Connect the conductance tester to the battery terminals (some testers require the removal of the battery cable for accuracy).

c. Follow the prompts on the conductance tester for the type and CCAs of the battery being tested.

d. Start the conductance test.

e. List the state of charge (usually a % of charge): _____ %

f. Record the available CCAs listed on the conductance tester: _____

5. Determine any necessary action(s):

6. Have your supervisor/instructor verify satisfactory completion of this procedure, any observations found, and any necessary action(s) recommended.

**Performance Rating**

CDX Tasksheet Number: C302

| 0 | 1 | 2 | 3 | 4 |
|---|---|---|---|---|

Supervisor/instructor signature _____ Date _____

▶ TASK  Confirm proper battery capacity for vehicle application;
perform battery capacity and load test; determine needed action.

**MAST**
*6B2*

Time off_____

Time on_____

Total time_____

**CDX Tasksheet Number: C818**

> **NOTE** The battery capacity test is also known as a load test or battery performance test. Follow all directions of the manufacturer whose tool you are using to load test the battery.

1. Research the specifications and procedures for testing the battery in the appropriate service information.
   a. What is the specified battery capacity for the vehicle you are working on?
      _____ CCA
   b. What type of battery is specified for this battery?
      Flooded cell: _____ AGM: _____ Other (list): _____

2. Inspect the battery and find its listed capacity rating: _____

3. Does this battery meet the specified CCA requirements for this vehicle?
   Yes: _____ No: _____

4. Determine the following load test variables for this battery:
   a. Required load test amps: _____ amps
   b. Required load test time (some testers are automatic):
      _____ seconds

5. Connect the load tester as directed by the equipment manufacturer. Make sure the tester clamps are secure on the battery terminals, and the inductive amps clamp is around the proper cable.

6. Load-test the battery. What was the battery minimum voltage (at the end of the load test time)? _____ volts

7. Did the battery pass the load test? Yes: _____ No: _____

8. If a battery fails the load test, what should be done next?

9. Determine any necessary action(s):

**10.** Have your supervisor/instructor verify satisfactory completion of this procedure, any observations found, and any necessary action(s) recommended.

**Performance Rating**

**CDX Tasksheet Number: C818**

| 0 | 1 | 2 | 3 | 4 |
|---|---|---|---|---|

Supervisor/instructor signature _____ Date _____

▶ **TASK** Identify electrical/electronic modules, security systems, radios, and other accessories that require reinitialization or code entry after reconnecting the vehicle battery.

**MAST**
*6B8*

**CDX Tasksheet Number: C645**

1. **Research the components that require reinitialization or code entry on the vehicle you are working on after reconnecting the battery. List those components here:**

2. **List the correct process for reinitialization or code entry for each of the components listed above:**

3. **Have your supervisor/instructor verify satisfactory completion of this procedure, any observations found, and any necessary action(s) recommended.**

**Performance Rating**

CDX Tasksheet Number: C645

| 0 | 1 | 2 | 3 | 4 |
|---|---|---|---|---|

Supervisor/instructor signature _____ Date _____

Time off_____

Time on_____

Total time_____

**CDX Tasksheet Number: C304**

1. Research the maintaining or restoring of electronic memory functions for this vehicle in the appropriate service information. Please follow all directions, and note that some vehicle electronic devices REQUIRE specific codes for reinitialization. If you don't have those codes available, do NOT disconnect the battery.

> **NOTE** Some manufacturers require the use of tools that help maintain memories, such as radios, adaptive strategies, etc. The use of these tools can minimize down time in restoring electronic memories lost when a battery is disconnected. In some cases, the use of a "memory minder," which is basically a battery that plugs into the 12V accessory socket or the data link connector, can be utilized. In all cases, follow the manufacturer's instructions.

2. Restore electronic memory functions.

   a. Change the vehicle's radio pre-set frequencies of the FM (1) stations and list those resets here:

      1. _____ 2. _____ 3. _____ 4. _____

   b. With NO memory minder installed, disconnect the negative battery terminal for at least 15 seconds.

   c. Reconnect the negative battery terminal, and tighten properly.

   d. Check the radio pre-sets. Did they change? Yes: _____ No: _____

      i. Why or why not?

   e. Restore the frequencies, as per manufacturer recommendations, to the stations noted in step 2a.

   f. What would you have to do to restore the vehicle's PCM adaptive learning memory if it is erased?

3. Maintain the electronic memory functions

   a. Reset the radio pre-sets to the same stations you did before.

   b. Install a memory minder to maintain electrical power in the system.

   c. Disconnect the negative battery terminal for at least 1 minute.

   d. Check the radio pre-sets. Did they change? Yes: _____ No: _____

      i. Why or why not?

e. Under this scenario, what happens to the vehicle's PCM adaptive learning memory if the battery is disconnected?

4. What did you learn?

5. Have your supervisor/instructor verify satisfactory completion of this procedure, any observations found, and any necessary action(s) recommended.

**Performance Rating**

**CDX Tasksheet Number: C304**

| 0 | 1 | 2 | 3 | 4 |
|---|---|---|---|---|

Supervisor/instructor signature _____ Date _____

Diagnose the cause(s) of excessive key-off battery drain
(parasitic draw); determine needed action.

**MAST**
6A8

**CDX Tasksheet Number: C817**

> **NOTE** Be sure to follow the correct steps for connecting your DMM to check for amperage/current flow. Have your supervisor/instructor check your connections. Improper connection of the DMM may damage your meter.

1. **Research key-off battery drain (parasitic drain) checks in the appropriate service information.**

    a. **List the maximum allowable key-off battery drain (parasitic drain) for the vehicle/simulator that has been assigned to you. What is the maximum allowable drain? _____ mA**

    b. **What is the specified time for the last module to go to sleep? _____ sec/min**

2. **List the appropriate steps to measure the key-off battery drain (parasitic drain):**

3. **Using the steps listed, measure the key off battery drain (parasitic drain):**

    a. **What is the actual drain? _____ mA**

    b. **Is this reading within specifications? Yes: _____ No: _____**

        i. **If no, identify the faulty circuit by pulling and replacing fuses one at a time. Watch the amps reading on the meter to see if it drops. If it drops substantially, you will want to investigate that circuit further, by disconnecting the loads and tracing the wires.**

4. **If pulling the fuses does not identify the faulty circuit, disconnect unfused wires one at a time, such as the alternator output wire and the ignition switch feed wire.**

5. **List the steps you took to diagnose the cause of the parasitic draw and their results:**

6. **Determine any necessary action(s):**

7. What would the customer concern be that would require you to perform this test?

8. Have your supervisor/instructor verify satisfactory completion of this procedure, any observations found, and any necessary action(s) recommended.

**CDX Tasksheet Number: C817**

| 0 | 1 | 2 | 3 | 4 |
|---|---|---|---|---|

Supervisor/instructor signature _____ Date _____

Time off_____

Time on_____

Total time_____

**CDX Tasksheet Number: N/A**

1. Determine what the impedance of the DMM is. List the impedance:
   _____ megohms (meter impedance)

2. Set the DMM to ohms and touch the leads together. This is the delta reading.
   List the reading: _____ ohms (Delta)

   Note: if the meter has a delta adjustment feature, press it so that the meter
   reads 0 ohms when the leads are touching. You won't have to worry about the
   delta reading in this case.

3. With the car off, and all doors closed, wait 30 seconds and then place the
   ohmmeter's black lead on the negative battery terminal and the red lead on the
   alternator case.

4. Read the ohmmeter and subtract the delta reading given previously. List the
   reading: _____ ohms (minus delta reading)

5. Compare this reading to the Chesney Parasitic Load Test graph. Approximately
   how many amps are draining? _____ mA

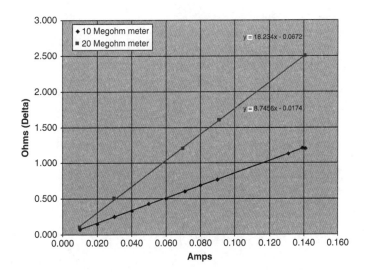

6. Is the reading within specifications?
   Yes: _____ No: _____

7. Open the driver's door and insure at least one dome light is on.

8. Place the black ohmmeter lead on the battery negative and the red lead on the
   alternator case.

9. Read the ohmmeter and subtract the delta reading given previously. List the reading: _____ ohms (minus delta reading)

10. Compare this reading to the Chesney Parasitic Load Test graph. Approximately how many amps are draining? _____ mA

11. Have your supervisor/instructor verify satisfactory completion of this procedure, any observations found, and any necessary action(s) recommended

**Performance Rating**

CDX Tasksheet Number: N/A

| 0 | 1 | 2 | 3 | 4 |
|---|---|---|---|---|

Supervisor/instructor signature _____ Date _____

**MAST**
*6C7*

**CDX Tasksheet Number: C1002**

1. **Research the description and operation of the automatic idle-stop/start-stop system. Describe in your own words how the automatic idle-stop/start-stop system operates:**

2. **Briefly describe the purpose of the automatic idle-stop/start-stop system:**

3. **Write a short description of the different types of idle-stop/start-stop systems used:**

4. **Have your supervisor/instructor verify satisfactory completion of your answers in steps 1-3.**

**Performance Rating**

CDX Tasksheet Number: C1002

| 0 | 1 | 2 | 3 | 4 |
|---|---|---|---|---|
| □ | □ | □ | □ | □ |

Supervisor/instructor signature _____ Date _____

**CDX Tasksheet Number: C309**

Time off_____

Time on_____

Total time_____

1.  **Research the specifications and procedures for performing starting system tests and repairs.**

    a.  **List the starter current draw specs:** _____ **amps at** _____ **volts (if listed)**

2.  **Connect the starting system tester as outlined in the appropriate service information.**

3.  **This test will require either the fuel system or ignition system to be disabled. Please follow the manufacturer's recommendations for disabling one of these two systems.**

4.  **Identify below which system was disabled and the steps you took to do this:**

5.  **Have your supervisor/instructor check your connections and how you disabled the fuel or ignition system(s).**

    a.  **Supervisor's/instructor's initials:** _____

6.  **Conduct the Starter Current Draw Test.**

    a.  **What was the current draw during the first second or two?**
        _____ **amps**
    b.  **What was the final current draw (after three or four seconds)?**
        _____ **amps**
    c.  **What was the lowest voltage during the test?** _____ **volts**

7.  **Compare your results to the manufacturer's specifications. List your observations:**

8.  **Determine any necessary action(s):**

9. **Have your supervisor/instructor verify satisfactory completion of this procedure, any observations found, and any necessary action(s) recommended.**

**Performance Rating**

CDX Tasksheet Number: C309

| 0 | 1 | 2 | 3 | 4 |
|---|---|---|---|---|

Supervisor/instructor signature _____ Date _____

Time off_____

Time on_____

Total time_____

**CDX Tasksheet Number: C310**

1.  Research the specifications and procedures for performing the starter circuit voltage drop tests in the appropriate service informaation.

    a.  What is the maximum starter circuit (high current cables) voltage drop specification(s) for this test?

        i.  Positive side: _____ volts

        ii. Negative (ground) side, if specified: _____ volts

2.  Disable the vehicle's fuel or ignition system so it will not start.

3.  Conduct the Starter Circuit Voltage Drop Test—Positive/Feed Side (heavy positive battery cable, not the control circuit).

    a.  List the voltmeter connection points in the circuit:

        DMM black lead: _____

        DMM red lead: _____

    b.  Conduct the Starter Circuit Voltage Drop Test:

        What is the voltage drop on the positive side? _____ volts

        Is this reading within specifications? Yes: _____ No: _____

4.  Conduct the Starter Circuit Voltage Drop Test—Ground Side.

    a.  List the voltmeter connection points in the circuit:

        DMM black lead: _____

        DMM red lead: _____

    b.  Conduct the Starter Circuit Voltage Drop Test:

        What is the voltage drop on the negative side? _____ volts

        Is this reading within specifications? Yes: _____ No: _____

5.  Determine any necessary action(s):

6.  Have your supervisor/instructor verify satisfactory completion of this procedure, any observations found, and any necessary action(s) recommended.

**Performance Rating**

**CDX Tasksheet Number: C310**

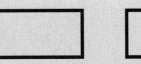

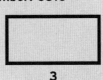
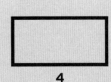

| 0 | 1 | 2 | 3 | 4 |

Supervisor/instructor signature _____ Date _____

▶ **TASK** Inspect and test starter relays and solenoids; determine needed action.

**MAST**
**6C3**

Time off_____

Time on_____

Total time_____

**CDX Tasksheet Number: C311**

1. Research the procedure and specifications for testing starter relays and solenoids in the appropriate service information.

    a. What is this vehicle's starting system equipped with?
       Starter Solenoid _____ ; Starter Relay _____ ; Both _____

    b. List the resistance of the starter solenoid windings: Pull in:
       _____ ohms;      hold in: _____ ohms

    c. List the specified resistance of the starter relay winding: _____ ohms

2. Disable the vehicle's fuel or ignition system so it will not start.

3. Following the manufacturer's test procedure, list the voltmeter connection points in the circuit to test the voltage drop across the relay or solenoid contacts.

    a. DMM red lead: _____

    b. DMM black lead: _____

4. Conduct the Starter Relay/Solenoid Voltage Drop Test.

    a. List the voltage drop: _____ volts

    b. Is this reading within specifications? Yes: _____ No: _____

5. Measure the resistance of the starter solenoid windings:

    a. Pull in: _____ ohms

    b. Hold in: _____ ohms

6. Measure the resistance of the starter relay winding: _____ ohms

7. Determine any necessary actions:

8. Have your supervisor/instructor verify satisfactory completion of this procedure, any observations found, and any necessary action(s) recommended.

© 2019 Jones & Bartlett Learning, LLC, an Ascend Learning Company

**Performance Rating**

**CDX Tasksheet Number: C311**

| 0 | 1 | 2 | 3 | 4 |
|---|---|---|---|---|
|   |   |   |   |   |

Supervisor/instructor signature _____ Date _____

Advanced Electrical/ Electronic Systems **191**

Time off_____

Time on_____

Total time_____

**CDX Tasksheet Number: C314**

**Vehicle used for this activity:**

Year _____ Make _____ Model_____

Odometer_____ VIN_____

1. **Locate a no-crank or slow-crank starting system symptom chart in the appropriate service information for the vehicle you are working on.**

   a. **Research the repair procedures for the condition of the vehicle, as outlined in the service information, for the vehicle assigned to you.**

2. **Most vehicles can be tested using the following procedure to determine whether the vehicle is experiencing an electrical or mechanical problem: Turn on the headlights and try to start the engine while listening to the starter and watching the headlights. Place a check mark next to the condition below that happened during this test.**

   a. **No starter noises and the headlights stayed at the same intensity: _____**

   > **NOTE** This fault is likely an electrical fault in the starter itself or the control circuit to the starter.

   b. **Loud single click when the key is turned to "crank" and headlights don't dim, or only dim slightly _____.**

   > **NOTE** This fault is likely an electrical fault caused by solenoid contacts or starter motor brushes that are excessively worn.

   c. **Loud repeated clicking "machine guns" when the key is turned to "crank": _____**

   > **NOTE** This fault is likely an electrical fault that may be caused by high resistance in the starter feed cable, a short circuit in the main starter feed cable after the starter relay, or the hold-in windings in the solenoid are open.

   d. **The starter engages and tries to crank, or cranks the engine slowly and the headlights went substantially dim:**

   > **NOTE** This fault could be an electrical fault or a mechanical fault. It may be caused by a discharged or weak battery, a shorted or dragging starter motor, or an engine that is mechanically bound up, such as from a hydro-locked cylinder, spun main bearing, or seized accessory drive on the engine. Turn the engine over by hand to determine if It is caused by a mechanical condition.

**e. The engine cranks substantially faster than normal:**

> **NOTE** This fault is likely a mechanical fault caused by low compression due to a broken or slipped timing belt/chain, bent valves, or piston rings that are not sealing.

3. Diagnose the problem based on these conditions. List the steps you took to diagnose the problem and the results you obtained:

4. Determine any necessary actions:

5. Have your supervisor/instructor verify satisfactory completion of this procedure, any observations found, and any necessary action(s) recommended.

**Performance Rating**

CDX Tasksheet Number: C314

|  |  |  |  |  |
|---|---|---|---|---|
| 0 | 1 | 2 | 3 | 4 |

Supervisor/instructor signature _____ Date _____

**MAST**
**6C4**

**CDX Tasksheet Number: C312**

1. Research the procedure and specifications for removing and installing the starter in the appropriate service information.

    a. List the specified starter mounting bolt torque: _____ ft-lb/N·m

    b. List the first step that should be performed prior to lifting the vehicle to remove the starter:

2. Remove the starter following the manufacturer's procedure.

    a. Have your supervisor/instructor verify the starter removal. Supervisor's/instructor's initials: _____

3. Inspect the gear teeth on the flywheel ring gear all the way around by turning the crankshaft by hand (ignition key "Off"). List your observations:

4. Install the starter following the manufacturer's procedures.

5. Restore the fuel system/ignition system to its proper operating condition. Start the vehicle and verify proper vehicle operation.

6. Have your supervisor/instructor verify satisfactory completion of this procedure, any observations found, and any necessary action(s) recommended.

**Performance Rating**

**CDX Tasksheet Number: C312**

| 0 | 1 | 2 | 3 | 4 |
|---|---|---|---|---|

Supervisor/instructor signature _____ Date _____

▶ TASK Inspect, adjust, and/or replace generator (alternator) drive belts; check pulleys and tensioners for wear; check pulley and belt alignment.

MAST
6D3

Time off_____

Time on_____

Total time_____

CDX Tasksheet Number: C317

1. Locate "inspecting, adjusting, and/or replacing generator (alternator) drive belts, pulleys, and tensioners; check pulley and belt alignment" in the appropriate service information for the vehicle you are working on.

   a. List the specified generator (alternator) drive belt tension:
   _____

   b. List the faults to look for when inspecting drive belts, pulleys, and tensioners:

   c. Describe how to check correct pulley and belt alignment:

   d. Locate the belt routing diagram or draw a picture of the current routing arrangement.

2. Install the fender covers.

3. Remove the vehicle drive belt(s).

4. Inspect the vehicle drive belts, pulleys, and tensioners for faults. List your observations for the following:

   a. Vehicle drive belt(s):

   b. Pulleys:

   c. Tensioners:

    **d. Pulley/belt alignment:**

5. **Have your instructor verify removal of belt(s) and faults found:**
   _____

6. **Reinstall the vehicle drive belts using the appropriate service information.**

7. **Re-tension the drive belt(s) using the appropriate service information.**

8. **Check for correct pulley, tensioner, and drive belt alignment.**

9. **Have your supervisor/instructor verify satisfactory completion of this procedure, any observations found, and any necessary action(s) recommended.**

**Performance Rating**

**CDX Tasksheet Number: C317**

| 0 | 1 | 2 | 3 | 4 |
|---|---|---|---|---|
|   |   |   |   |   |

Supervisor/instructor signature _____ Date _____

**MAST**
6D1

Time off_____

Time on_____

Total time_____

**CDX Tasksheet Number: C315**

1. Research "performing a charging system output test" in the appropriate service information for the vehicle you are working on. What is the specified charging system output? _____ amps at _____ volts at _____ rpm

2. Install the fender covers, exhaust hose(s), and wheel chocks, and set the parking brake.

3. Connect the charging system tester as outlined in the appropriate service information.
   a. Heavy red lead to the battery positive terminal
   b. Heavy black lead to the battery negative terminal
   c. Green/Black amps clamp around alternator output wire (facing the correct direction)

4. Have your supervisor/instructor verify your test procedure and connections. Supervisor's/instructor's initials: _____

5. Conduct the charging system output test. List the measured results at the maximum output: _____ amps at _____ volts at _____ engine rpm

6. Compare your results to the manufacturer's specifications. List your observations:

7. Determine any necessary action(s):

8. Have your supervisor/instructor verify satisfactory completion of this procedure, any observations found, and any necessary action(s) recommended.

**Performance Rating**

**CDX Tasksheet Number: C315**

| 0 | 1 | 2 | 3 | 4 |
|---|---|---|---|---|

Supervisor/instructor signature _____ Date _____

Perform charging circuit voltage drop tests;
determine needed action.

**CDX Tasksheet Number: C319**

1.  **Research the procedure and specifications for performing the charging circuit voltage drop tests in the appropriate service information.**

    a.  **List the maximum allowable voltage drop (generator output terminal to battery positive post): _____ volts**

    b.  **List the maximum allowable voltage drop (generator housing to battery negative post): _____ volts**

2.  **Install the fender covers, exhaust hose(s), and wheel chocks, and set the parking brake.**

3.  **Connect the DMM as outlined in the appropriate service information.**

    a.  **List the points that each voltmeter test lead should be connected to, to test the voltage drop between the output terminal of the alternator and the positive post of the battery:**

    i.  **DMM black lead: _____**

    ii. **DMM red lead: _____**

    b.  **List the points that each voltmeter test lead should be connected to, to test the voltage drop between the housing of the alternator and the negative post of the battery:**

    i.  **DMM black lead: _____**

    ii. **DMM red lead: _____**

4.  **Have your supervisor/instructor verify your test procedure and connections. Supervisor's/instructor's initials: _____**

5.  **Conduct the charging system voltage drop test. List the measured results:**

    a.  **Voltage drop between the alternator output terminal and battery positive post is: _____ V at: _____ A**

    b.  **Voltage drop between the alternator housing and battery negative post is: _____ V at: _____ A**

6.  **Compare your results to the manufacturer's specifications. List your observations:**

7.  **Determine any necessary action(s):**

8. Have your supervisor/instructor verify satisfactory completion of this procedure, any observations found, and any necessary action(s) recommended.

**Performance Rating**

| 0 | 1 | 2 | 3 | 4 |

Supervisor/instructor signature _____ Date _____

Diagnose (troubleshoot) charging system for the cause of undercharge, no-charge, and overcharge conditions.

**MAST**
**6D2**

Time off_____

Time on_____

Total time_____

**CDX Tasksheet Number: C316**

1. Research the following specifications in the appropriate service information for the vehicle assigned.

> **NOTE** Some charging systems use variable charging modes depending on the conditions present, such as battery temperature, driving condition, etc. Make sure you follow the manufacturer's specified testing procedures when testing these systems.

   a. Rated output for the alternator being tested: _____ amps
   b. Regulated voltage: _____ volts
   c. How is the alternator full fielded on this vehicle?

2. Install the exhaust hose(s) and wheel chocks, and set the parking brake.

3. Connect the charging system tester as outlined in the appropriate service information.

4. Test the maximum current output of the alternator. List reading here: _____ amps

5. Using the diode/stator setting or AC ripple setting, test the integrity of the diodes and stator. List the results:

6. Conduct the charging system regulated voltage test. Do this by measuring the maximum voltage that the charging system achieves while the engine runs at approximately 1500 rpm and waiting until the voltage doesn't rise any further. Do NOT allow the voltage to exceed 16 volts. Regulated voltage: _____ V

7. Compare your results to the manufacturer's specifications. List your observations:

8. Determine any necessary action(s):

9. Have your supervisor/instructor verify satisfactory completion of this procedure, any observations found, and any necessary action(s) recommended.

**Performance Rating**

**CDX Tasksheet Number: C316**

| | | | | |
|---|---|---|---|---|
| ☐ | ☐ | ☐ | ☐ | ☐ |
| 0 | 1 | 2 | 3 | 4 |

Supervisor/instructor signature _____ Date _____

MAST
6D4

**CDX Tasksheet Number: C318**

1. **Research the procedure for removing, inspecting and installing a generator (alternator) in the appropriate service information. List any precautions:**

2. **Disconnect battery negative terminal (consider using a memory minder while doing this task).**

3. **Remove the generator (alternator) as per the service information.**

4. **Inspect the generator (alternator) as per the service procedure. List any faults or defects found:**

   a. **Determine any necessary action(s):**

5. **Have your supervisor/instructor verify removal of generator (alternator). Supervisor's/instructor's initials: _____**

6. **Install the generator (alternator) as per the service information and properly tension the belt(s).**

7. **Start the engine to make sure everything is operating correctly. List your observations:**

8. **Have your supervisor/instructor verify satisfactory completion of this procedure, any observations found, and any necessary action(s) recommended.**

**Performance Rating**

CDX Tasksheet Number: C318

| 0 | 1 | 2 | 3 | 4 |
|---|---|---|---|---|

Supervisor/instructor signature _____ Date _____

**TASK** Identify system voltage and safety precautions
associated with high-intensity discharge headlights.

**MAST**
*6E4*

**CDX Tasksheet Number: C564**

1. **Using appropriate service information, identify system voltage and safety precautions associated with high-intensity discharge (HID) headlights.**

   a. **HID lamp voltage:** _____ **volts**
   b. **List the safety precautions required when working on HID system:**

2. **Have your supervisor/instructor verify satisfactory completion of this task.**

**Performance Rating**

CDX Tasksheet Number: C564

| 0 | 1 | 2 | 3 | 4 |
|---|---|---|---|---|

Supervisor/instructor signature _____ Date _____

Time off_____

Time on_____

Total time_____

**CDX Tasksheet Number: C321**

1. Research the headlamp or exterior lighting section in the appropriate service information for the vehicle you are working on.

   a. Type of headlights vehicle is equipped with: _____

   b. High-beam bulb number: _____

   c. Low-beam bulb number: _____

2. Research the headlamp aiming process in the appropriate service information for the vehicle you are working on. List (or print off and attach) the steps that are required to aim these headlamps:

> **NOTE** Do not touch the bulb with your fingers. Some bulbs will fail prematurely due to the oils from your skin.

3. Aim the headlamps following the specified procedure.

4. List any challenges you had performing this task:

5. Have your supervisor/instructor verify satisfactory completion of this procedure.

**Performance Rating**

**CDX Tasksheet Number: C321**

| 0 | 1 | 2 | 3 | 4 |
|---|---|---|---|---|
|   |   |   |   |   |

Supervisor/instructor signature _____ Date _____

► **TASK** Diagnose (troubleshoot) the cause of incorrect operation
of warning devices and other driver information systems;
determine needed action.

**MAST**
6F2

**CDX Tasksheet Number: C325**

**Vehicle used for this activity:**

Year _____ Make _____ Model_____

Odometer_____ VIN_____

1. **List the customer concern/complaint regarding incorrect operation of warning devices and other driver information systems:**

2. **Research the particular complaint/concern in the appropriate service information. List the possible causes:**

   a. **List any relevant specifications:**

3. **Diagnose the cause of the concern/complaint using the service information and wiring diagrams. List your tests and their results:**

4. **List the cause of the concern/complaint:**

5. **Determine any needed action(s) to correct the fault:**

6. Have your supervisor/instructor verify satisfactory completion of this procedure, any observations found, and any needed action(s) recommended.

**Performance Rating**

CDX Tasksheet Number: C325

| | | | | |
|---|---|---|---|---|
| 0 | 1 | 2 | 3 | 4 |

Supervisor/instructor signature _____ Date _____

Inspect and test gauges and gauge sending units for cause of abnormal gauge readings; determine needed action.

**MAST**
6F1

Time off_____

Time on_____

Total time_____

**CDX Tasksheet Number: C646**

1. List the customer concern/complaint regarding abnormal gauge readings:

2. Research the particular complaint/concern in the appropriate service information. List the possible causes:

    a. List any relevant gauge or sending unit specifications:

3. Diagnose the cause of the concern/complaint using the service information and wiring diagrams. List your tests and their results:

4. List the cause of the concern/complaint:

5. Determine any needed action(s) to correct the fault:

6. Have your supervisor/instructor verify satisfactory completion of this procedure, any observations found, and any needed action(s) recommended.

**Performance Rating**

CDX Tasksheet Number: C646

| | | | | |
|---|---|---|---|---|
| 0 | 1 | 2 | 3 | 4 |

Supervisor/instructor signature _____ Date _____

Reset maintenance indicators as required.

Time off_____

Time on_____

Total time_____

**CDX Tasksheet Number: C1003**

1.  Research the description and operation of each maintenance indicator and the procedure for resetting the maintenance indicators in the appropriate service information. List each of the maintenance indicators and the reset procedure:

2.  Turn the ignition switch to the on/run position (Key On, Engine Off-KOEO). List the status of each maintenance indicator:

3.  Start the engine and allow it to run for a few minutes. List the status of each maintenance indicator:

4.  List any maintenance indicators that are showing required maintenance:

5.  Ask your supervisor/instructor if you should carry out the reset procedure for any maintenance indicators that are showing required maintenance.

6. Have your supervisor/instructor verify satisfactory completion of this procedure, any observations found, and any necessary action(s) recommended.

**Performance Rating**

CDX Tasksheet Number: C1003

| | | | | |
|---|---|---|---|---|
| 0 | 1 | 2 | 3 | 4 |

Supervisor/instructor signature _____ Date _____

Diagnose (troubleshoot) the cause of brighter-than-normal, intermittent, dim, or no-light operation; determine needed action.

**MAST**
6E1

Time off_____

Time on_____

Total time_____

**CDX Tasksheet Number: C320**

**Vehicle used for this activity:**

Year _____ Make _____ Model_____

Odometer_____ VIN_____

1.  **List the customer complaint/concern regarding the lighting system fault:**

2.  **If the lights are dim or do not operate, go to step 3. If the lights are too bright, go to step 9.**

3.  **Research the affected lighting system troubleshooting section and the wiring diagram(s) in the appropriate service information for the vehicle you are working on.**

4.  **Turn on the affected light(s), measure the battery voltage, and list it here: _____ volts**

5.  **Measure the voltage across the power and ground at the light (light illuminated). List the voltage: _____ volts**

    a.  **Calculate the total voltage drop in the circuit and list it here: _____ volt drop**
    b.  **Is the voltage drop excessive? Yes: _____ No: _____**
    c.  **If yes, go to step 7. If no, go to step 6.**

6.  **Inspect the bulb and connections for any faults (wrong bulb, corroded, or loose connection). List your observations:**

7.  **Measure the voltage drop from the battery positive post to the input terminal of the light.**

    a.  **List the voltage drop: _____ volts**
    b.  **Is this within specifications? Yes: _____ No: _____**
    c.  **Determine any necessary action(s):**

8. Measure the voltage drop from the bulb ground to the battery negative post.

    a. List the voltage drop: _____ volts

    b. Is this within specifications? Yes: _____ No: _____

    c. Determine any necessary action(s):

9. Install exhaust hose(s) and wheel chocks, and set the parking brake. Start the vehicle.

10. Measure the charging system voltage at the battery, with the engine running at 1500 rpm: _____ volts

    a. Is this within specification? Yes: _____ No: _____

> **NOTE** If the battery voltage is too high, you will need to perform charging system checks to determine the cause of the overcharge.

11. List your observations:

12. Determine any necessary action(s):

13. Have your supervisor/instructor verify satisfactory completion of this procedure, any observations found, and any necessary action(s) recommended.

**Performance Rating**

CDX Tasksheet Number: C320

| 0 | 1 | 2 | 3 | 4 |
|---|---|---|---|---|
|   |   |   |   |   |

Supervisor/instructor signature _____ Date _____

▶ **TASK** Inspect interior and exterior lamps and sockets
including headlights and auxiliary lights
(fog lights/driving lights); replace as needed.

Time off_____

Time on_____

Total time_____

**CDX Tasksheet Number: C956**

1. **Inspect the operation of the following interior lights (vehicles have different arrangements, so find as many as possible). List your observations for each light listed:**

   a. **Dome:** _____

   b. **Map:** _____

   c. **Dash:** _____

   d. **Kick panel:** _____

   e. **Glove box:** _____

   f. **Vanity mirror:** _____

   g. **Rear passenger:** _____

   h. **Other:** _____

2. **Inspect the operation of the following exterior lights (vehicles have different arrangements, so find as many as possible):**

   a. **Rear tail:** _____

   b. **License:** _____

   c. **Rear-side marker:** _____

   d. **Brake:** _____

   e. **Center high-mount stoplight:** _____

   f. **Back-up:** _____

   g. **Front park:** _____

   h. **Front-side marker:** _____

   i. **Low beam:** _____

   j. **High beam:** _____

   k. **Fog:** _____

   l. **Driving:** _____

   m. **Cornering:** _____

   n. **Clearance:** _____

   o. **Under-hood:** _____

   p. **Trunk:** _____

   q. **Other:** _____

3. **Ask your instructor which bulbs he/she would like you to remove. List them here:**

4. **List the name of the light and the bulb number for each bulb you removed:**

5. Inspect/clean the sockets for each bulb you removed.

6. Ask your supervisor/instructor if you should apply dielectric grease to the socket of the bulb you have removed.

7. Reinstall the bulb into the socket and reinstall any other pieces that were removed to gain access to the bulb.

8. Have your supervisor/instructor verify satisfactory completion of this procedure.

**Performance Rating**

CDX Tasksheet Number: C956

| | | | | |
|---|---|---|---|---|
| 0 | 1 | 2 | 3 | 4 |

Supervisor/instructor signature _____ Date _____

**► TASK** Diagnose operation of entertainment and related circuits (such as: radio, DVD, remote CD changer, navigation, amplifiers, speakers, antennas, and voice-activated accessories); determine needed repairs.

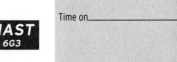

Time off_____

Time on_____

Total time_____

**CDX Tasksheet Number: C336**

**Vehicle used for this activity:**

Year _____ Make _____ Model_____

Odometer_____ VIN_____

1. **Ask your instructor to assign a vehicle with a fault in the radio or entertainment system.**

2. **List the customer concern/complaint:**

3. **Locate the diagnostic procedure for the related customer concern/complaint in the appropriate service information for the vehicle you are working on. Briefly describe the diagnostic procedure for the fault (or attach diagnosis printout):**

4. **Following the specified procedure, diagnose the related customer concern/ complaint.  List your tests and their results:**

5. **List the cause of the customer concern/complaint:**

6. **Determine any needed repair(s) to correct the customer concern/complaint:**

© 2019 Jones & Bartlett Learning, LLC, an Ascend Learning Company

7. Have your supervisor/instructor verify satisfactory completion of this procedure, any observations found, and any needed repair(s) recommended.

**Performance Rating**

CDX Tasksheet Number: C336

| | | | | |
|---|---|---|---|---|
| 0 | 1 | 2 | 3 | 4 |

Supervisor/instructor signature _____ Date _____

Identify hybrid vehicle A/C system electrical circuits
and the service/safety precautions.

Time off_____

Time on_____

**CDX Tasksheet Number: C827**

Total time_____

**Vehicle used for this activity:**

Year _____ Make _____ Model_____

Odometer_____ VIN_____

1. **Research the description and operation of a hybrid vehicle A/C system in the appropriate service information.**

    a. **What powers the A/C compressor (prime mover)?**

    b. **Does the manufacturer use a special designation for the A/C system electrical circuits? Yes: _____ No: _____**
       **i. If yes, what is it?**

    c. **List the voltage(s) that the A/C system electrical circuits operate on:**

    d. **How is the A/C compressor driven? V belt: _____ Serpentine belt: _____ Direct drive: _____ Other (specify below)**
       **i. Specified refrigerant: _____**

       **ii. Refrigerant capacity: _____ lb/kg**

       **iii. Specified lubricant: _____**

       **iv. Lubricant capacity: _____ oz/mL**

       **v. List the specified safety precautions when servicing this system:**

2. Have your supervisor/instructor verify satisfactory completion of this procedure, any observations found, and any necessary action(s) recommended.

**Performance Rating**

CDX Tasksheet Number: C827

| 0 | 1 | 2 | 3 | 4 |
|---|---|---|---|---|

Supervisor/instructor signature _____ Date _____

Check operation of automatic or semi-automatic
HVAC control systems; determine needed action.

**MAST**
**7D8**

Time off_____

Time on_____

Total time_____

**CDX Tasksheet Number: C866**

**Vehicle used for this activity:**

Year _____ Make _____ Model_____

Odometer_____ VIN_____

1. **Research the description and operation of the HVAC climate control system in the appropriate service information.**

   a. **Is this system a full-authority climate control system? Yes: _____**
   **No: _____**

   b. **If equipped, how do you test the evaporator thermistors?**

   c. **If equipped, how do you test the three-wire A/C pressure sensors?**

   d. **If equipped, how do you access the trouble codes on this vehicle?**

   e. **How is the heater controlled? Heater control valve: _____ Blend door: _____**

   f. **Research the steps to test the operation of the climate control system:**

2. **Following the specified procedure, test the operation of the climate control system. List your steps and the results:**

3. **Determine any necessary action(s):**

4. **Have your supervisor/instructor verify satisfactory completion of this procedure, any observations found, and any necessary action(s) recommended.**

**Performance Rating**

CDX Tasksheet Number: C866

| 0 | 1 | 2 | 3 | 4 |
|---|---|---|---|---|

Supervisor/instructor signature _____ Date _____

Using a scan tool, observe and record related HVAC data
and trouble codes.

**MAST**
**7A9**

Time off_____

Time on_____

Total time_____

**CDX Tasksheet Number: C566**

**Vehicle used for this activity:**

Year _____ Make _____ Model_____

Odometer_____ VIN_____

1. **List the HVAC-related customer concern:**

2. **Start the vehicle and operate the HVAC system to verify the concern. List your observation(s):**

3. **Following the specified procedure, connect a scan tool to the vehicle. Obtain and record the following information.**

   a. **HVAC-related trouble code(s) and their description(s):**

   b. **HVAC-related data (list at least three readings and their descriptions):**

4. **Have your supervisor/instructor verify satisfactory completion of this procedure, any observations found, and any necessary action(s) recommended.**

**Performance Rating**

**CDX Tasksheet Number: C566**

| 0 | 1 | 2 | 3 | 4 |
|---|---|---|---|---|
|   |   |   |   |   |

Supervisor/instructor signature _____ Date _____

Inspect and test HVAC system control panel assembly; determine needed action.

**MAST**
7D4

Time off_____

Time on_____

Total time_____

**CDX Tasksheet Number: C376**

**Vehicle used for this activity:**

Year _____ Make _____ Model_____

Odometer_____ VIN_____

1. List the A/C-heater control panel–related HVAC customer concern:

2. Verify the concern by operating each of the control panel controls through their range and list your observation(s):

3. Research the procedure and specifications for inspecting and testing the A/C-heater control panel in the appropriate service information.

    a. What kind of controls is this vehicle equipped with? _____
    b. List or print off and attach to this sheet the steps to inspect and test the control panel:

4. Following the specified procedure, inspect and test the control panel. List your tests and results:

5. List the cause of the concern:

6. Determine any necessary action(s) to correct the fault:

7. Have your supervisor/instructor verify satisfactory completion of this procedure, any observations found, and any necessary action(s) recommended.

**Performance Rating**

**CDX Tasksheet Number: C376**

| 0 | 1 | 2 | 3 | 4 |
|---|---|---|---|---|

Supervisor/instructor signature _____ Date _____

**▶ TASK** Inspect and test HVAC system control cables, motors, and linkages; perform needed action.

**MAST 7D5**

Time off_____

Time on_____

Total time_____

**CDX Tasksheet Number: C865**

**Vehicle used for this activity:**

Year _____ Make _____ Model_____

Odometer_____ VIN_____

1. **Research the procedures and specifications to inspect and test the control cables, motors, and linkages in the appropriate service information.**

   a. **List any precautions for this task:**

   b. **List or print off and attach to this sheet any procedures and specifications for this task:**

2. **Verify the operation of all HVAC control cables, motors, and linkages. List your observation(s):**

3. **Following the specified procedure, inspect and test the cables, motors, and linkages. List your tests and results:**

4. **Determine any necessary action(s):**

5. **Have your supervisor/instructor verify satisfactory completion of this procedure, any observations found, and any necessary action(s) recommended.**

© 2019 Jones & Bartlett Learning, LLC, an Ascend Learning Company

**Performance Rating**

**CDX Tasksheet Number: C865**

| 0 | 1 | 2 | 3 | 4 |
|---|---|---|---|---|

Supervisor/instructor signature _____ Date _____

Advanced Electrical/ Electronic Systems **231**

Diagnose temperature control problems in the HVAC
system; determine needed action.

**MAST**
7C3

**CDX Tasksheet Number: C362**

1. **List the heater/ventilation-related customer concern:**

2. **Research the customer concern in the appropriate service information. List the possible causes:**

3. **Following the specified procedure, diagnose the customer concern. List your tests and observations:**

4. **List the cause of the customer concern:**

5. **Determine any necessary action(s) to correct the fault:**

6. **Have your supervisor/instructor verify satisfactory completion of this procedure, any observations found, and any necessary action(s) recommended.**

© 2019 Jones & Bartlett Learning, LLC, an Ascend Learning Company

**Performance Rating**

CDX Tasksheet Number: C362

| 0 | 1 | 2 | 3 | 4 |
|---|---|---|---|---|

Supervisor/instructor signature _____ Date _____

**TASK** Inspect HVAC system ducts, doors, hoses, cabin filters, and outlets; perform needed action.

**MAST**
7D6

Time off_____

Time on_____

Total time_____

**CDX Tasksheet Number: C378**

**Vehicle used for this activity:**

Year _____ Make _____ Model _____

Odometer _____ VIN _____

1. **Research the procedure and specifications for inspecting the above components in the appropriate service information.**

    a. **Is this vehicle equipped with a cabin air filter? Yes:** _____
       **No:** _____

    b. **What is the recommended replacement interval for the cabin air filter?**
       _____ **mi/km/mo**

2. **Following the specified procedure, inspect the following components. List your observations below.**

    a. **Ducts:**

    b. **Doors:**

    c. **Hoses:**

    d. **Cabin filter(s):**

    e. **Outlets:**

3. **Determine any necessary action(s):**

4. **Have your supervisor/instructor verify satisfactory completion of this procedure, any observations found, and any necessary action(s) recommended.**

**Performance Rating**

**CDX Tasksheet Number: C378**

| 0 | 1 | 2 | 3 | 4 |
|---|---|---|---|---|

Supervisor/instructor signature _____ Date _____

**▶ TASK** Inspect and test HVAC system blower, motors, resistors, switches, relays, wiring, and protection devices; determine needed action.

**MAST 7D1**

Time off_____

Time on_____

Total time_____

**CDX Tasksheet Number: C373**

**Vehicle used for this activity:**

Year _____ Make _____ Model_____

Odometer_____ VIN_____

1. **Research the procedure and specifications to inspect and test the electrical components of the HVAC system in the appropriate service information.**

    a. **Specified resistance of the blower motor:** _____ ohms
    b. **Specified resistance of the blower motor resistors**
    Resistance on the highest resisted speed: _____ ohms
    Resistance on medium-high resisted speed: _____ ohms
    Resistance on medium-low resisted speed: _____ ohms
    Resistance on the lowest resisted speed: _____ ohms

    c. **List all the protection devices for the blower motor circuit:**

2. **Following the specified procedure, inspect and test the following devices. List your observations below.**

    a. **Blower motor:**

    b. **Blower motor resistors:**

    c. **Appropriate switches:**

    d. **Appropriate relays:**

© 2019 Jones & Bartlett Learning, LLC, an Ascend Learning Company

     e.  **Appropriate circuit protection devices:**

     f.  **Appropriate wiring harness:**

3.  **Determine any necessary action(s):**

4.  **Have your supervisor/instructor verify satisfactory completion of this procedure, any observations found, and any necessary action(s) recommended.**

**Performance Rating**

CDX Tasksheet Number: C373

| 0 | 1 | 2 | 3 | 4 |
|---|---|---|---|---|
|   |   |   |   |   |

Supervisor/instructor signature _____ Date _____

Diagnose A/C compressor clutch control systems; determine needed action.

Time off_____

Time on_____

Total time_____

**CDX Tasksheet Number: C374**

**Vehicle used for this activity:**

Year _____ Make _____ Model_____

Odometer_____ VIN_____

1. **Research the procedure and specifications to inspect and test the electrical components of the A/C compressor clutch control system in the appropriate service information.**

   a. Specified resistance of the clutch winding: _____ ohms

   b. A/C cycling switch specifications (if equipped)
      Off pressure: _____ psi/kPa
      On pressure: _____ psi/kPa

   c. A/C thermoswitch specifications (if equipped)
      Off temperature: _____ °F/°C
      On temperature: _____ °F/°C

   d. A/C duct temperature specifications: _____ °F/°C

   e. A/C high-pressure cut-out switch specifications
      Off pressure: _____ psi/kPa
      On pressure: _____ psi/kPa

   f. A/C low pressure cut-out switch (non-cycling) (if equipped)
      Off pressure: _____ psi/kPa
      On pressure: _____ psi/kPa

   g. A/C compressor clutch relay specifications (if equipped)
      Relay winding resistance: _____ ohms
      Maximum allowable voltage drop across relay contacts:
      _____ volts

   h. List all the fuses and/or fusible links for the A/C compressor clutch circuit:



   i. Does the compressor clutch share a fuse with the blower circuit?
      Yes: _____ No: _____

2. **Following the specified procedure, activate the A/C system.**

   a. Does the compressor clutch engage? Yes: _____ No: _____

   b. If yes, continue on to step 3. If no, skip to step 5.



3. **List your observations below.**

   a. A/C cycling switch readings (if equipped)
      Off pressure: _____ psi/kPa
      On pressure: _____ psi/kPa

   b. A/C thermoswitch readings (if equipped)
      Off temperature: _____ °F/°C
      On temperature: _____ °F/°C

   c. A/C duct temperature: _____ °F/°C

d. A/C high pressure cut-out switch readings (may require condenser airflow blockage to test). (DUE TO THE SAFETY IMPLICATIONS, ONLY PERFORM THIS TEST IF APPROVED BY YOUR SUPERVISOR/INSTRUCTOR.)

Off pressure: _____ psi/kPa

On pressure: _____ psi/kPa

e. Determine any necessary action(s):

4. **Have your supervisor/instructor verify the readings. Supervisor's/instructor's initials:** _____

> **NOTE** If your instructor signed off on this step, skip to the final check off.

5. **If the clutch does not engage, install a gauge set and check for minimum refrigerant pressure. If pressure is insufficient, check for refrigerant leaks, then retest after repair. If pressure is sufficient, measure the voltage applied to the compressor clutch winding.**

   a. Applied voltage to the compressor clutch: _____ volts

   b. Compressor clutch winding resistance: _____ ohms

   c. A/C compressor clutch relay readings

   Relay winding resistance: _____ ohms

   Voltage at the relay contact input terminal: _____ volts

   Voltage drop across relay contacts (A/C on): _____ volts

   d. Describe the circuit protection device(s) condition:

6. **Determine any necessary action(s):**

> **NOTE** If repairs are made, return to step 3 and retest.

7. **Have your supervisor/instructor verify satisfactory completion of this procedure, any observations found, and any necessary action(s) recommended.**

**Performance Rating**

CDX Tasksheet Number: C374

| 0 | 1 | 2 | 3 | 4 |
|---|---|---|---|---|

Supervisor/instructor signature _____ Date _____

© 2019 Jones & Bartlett Learning, LLC, an Ascend Learning Company

**240** Advanced Electrical/Electronic Systems

Diagnose malfunctions in the vacuum, mechanical, and electrical
components and controls of the heating, ventilation, and
A/C (HVAC) system; determine needed action.

**MAST**
**7D3**

Time off_____

Time on_____

Total time_____

**CDX Tasksheet Number: C835**

**Vehicle used for this activity:**

Year _____ Make _____ Model_____

Odometer_____ VIN_____

1. **List the vacuum, mechanical, or electrical controls–related HVAC customer concern:**

2. **Verify the concern by operating each of the HVAC vacuum, mechanical, and electrical controls through their range and list your observation(s):**

3. **Research the procedure, specifications, and wiring diagrams for diagnosing the concern in the appropriate service information.**
    a. **List the possible faults:**

    b. **List or print off and attach to this sheet the steps to diagnose the fault:**

4. **Following the specified procedure, diagnose the concern. List your tests and the results:**

5. **List the cause of the concern:**

6. **Determine any necessary action(s) to correct the fault:**

7. **Have your supervisor/instructor verify satisfactory completion of this procedure, any observations found, and any necessary action(s) recommended.**

**Performance Rating**

**CDX Tasksheet Number: C835**

| 0 | 1 | 2 | 3 | 4 |
|---|---|---|---|---|

Supervisor/instructor signature _____ Date _____

# Appendix: CDX/NATEF Correlation Guide

| CDX Tasksheet Number | 2017 MAST NATEF Reference and Priority | Corresponding Page(s) |
| --- | --- | --- |
| C387 | 8A2; P-1 | 1 |
| NN08 | N/A | 3-4 |
| C386 | 8A1; P-1 | 5-6 |
| C422 | 8D4; P-2 | 7-8 |
| C868 | 8D3; P-1 | 9-10 |
| C420 | 8D2; P-2 | 11-12 |
| C842 | 8D7; P-2 | 13-14 |
| C713 | 8D1; P-2 | 15-16 |
| C962 | 8D5; P-1 | 17 |
| C424 | 8D6; P-2 | 19 |
| C665 | 8D8; P-1 | 21-22 |
| C428 | 8D9; P-1 | 23-24 |
| C963 | 8D10; P-1 | 25 |
| C429 | 8D11; P-2 | 27 |
| C869 | 8D13; P-2 | 29 |
| C965 | 8D12; P-2 | 31 |
| C714 | 8E6; P-2 | 33-34 |
| C844 | 8E5; P-1 | 35-36 |
| C666 | 8E1; P-3 | 37-38 |
| C432 | 8E2; P-2 | 39-40 |
| C391 | 8A4; P-2 | 41-42 |
| C667 | 8E3; P-2 | 43-46 |
| C843 | 8E4; P-2 | 47-48 |
| C827 | 7B4; P-2 | 49-50 |
| C561 | 6B7; P-2 | 51 |
| C900 | 1A9; P-2 | 53 |
| C874 | 6B9; P-2 | 55 |

## Section AT 204: Driveability and Diagnosis

| CDX Tasksheet Number | 2017 MAST NATEF Reference and Priority | Corresponding Page(s) |
|---|---|---|
| C387 | 8A2; P-1 | 57 |
| NN08 | N/A | 59-60 |
| C386 | 8A1; P-1 | 61-62 |
| NN09 | N/A | 63 |
| C392 | 8A5; P-1 | 65 |
| C393 | 8A6; P-2 | 67-68 |
| C709 | 8A7; P-1 | 69-70 |
| C395 | 8A8; P-1 | 71 |
| C390 | 8A3; P-3 | 73-74 |
| C004 | 1A4; P-1 | 75-76 |
| C400 | 8A11; P-1 | 77 |
| C398 | 8A10; P-1 | 79-80 |
| C841 | 8B2; P-1 | 81 |
| C960 | 8C4; P-1 | 83-84 |
| C712 | 8C1; P-2 | 85-86 |
| C663 | 8C2; P-1 | 87-88 |
| C664 | 8C3; P-3 | 89-90 |
| C710 | 8A9; P-2 | 91 |
| C661 | 8B4; P-1 | 93 |
| C659 | 8B1; P-1 | 95 |
| C840 | 8B7; P-2 | 97-98 |
| C867 | 8B3; P-1 | 99 |
| C668 | 8E7; P-2 | 101-102 |
| C660 | 8B5; P-1 | 103-104 |
| C711 | 8B6; P-1 | 105-106 |
| C409 | 8B8; P-2 | 107-108 |

## Section AT 209: Advanced Electrical/ Electronic Systems

| CDX Tasksheet Number | 2017 MAST NATEF Reference and Priority | Corresponding Page(s) |
|---|---|---|
| C952 | 6A7; P-1 | 109-110 |
| C299 | 6A10; P-1 | 111-112 |
| C955 | 6A12; P-1 | 113 |
| C641 | 6A3; P-1 | 115 |
| C291 | 6A5; P-1 | 117-118 |
| C295 | 6A6; P-1 | 119-120 |
| C298 | 6A9; P-1 | 121-122 |

| CDX Tasksheet Number | 2017 MAST NATEF Reference and Priority | Corresponding Page(s) |
| --- | --- | --- |
| C313 | 6C5; P-2 | 123-124 |
| C642 | 6A11; P-2 | 125-126 |
| C661 | 8B4; P-1 | 127 |
| C659 | 8B1; P-1 | 129 |
| C840 | 8B7; P-2 | 131-132 |
| C867 | 8B3; P-1 | 133 |
| C668 | 8E7; P-2 | 135-136 |
| C660 | 8B5; P-1 | 137-138 |
| C711 | 8B6; P-1 | 139-140 |
| C409 | 8B8; P-2 | 141-142 |
| C338 | 6G5; P-2 | 143 |
| C649 | 6G6; P-2 | 145-146 |
| C327 | 6G4; P-1 | 147-148 |
| C340 | 6G2; P-2 | 149-150 |
| C330 | 6G1; P-2 | 151-152 |
| C387 | 8A2; P-1 | 153 |
| C841 | 8B2; P-1 | 155 |
| C960 | 8C4; P-1 | 157-158 |
| C386 | 8A1; P-1 | 159-160 |
| C712 | 8C1; P-2 | 161-162 |
| C663 | 8C2; P-1 | 163-164 |
| C664 | 8C3; P-3 | 165-166 |
| C819 | 6B5; P-1 | 167-168 |
| C820 | 6B6; P-1 | 169 |
| C644 | 6B4; P-1 | 171-172 |
| C302 | 6B1; P-1 | 173-174 |
| C818 | 6B2; P-1 | 175-176 |
| C645 | 6B8; P-1 | 177 |
| C304 | 6B3; P-1 | 179-180 |
| C817 | 6A8; P-1 | 181-182 |
| NN12 | N/A | 183-184 |
| C1002 | 6C7; P-2 | 185 |
| C309 | 6C1; P-1 | 187-188 |
| C310 | 6C2; P-1 | 189 |
| C311 | 6C3; P-2 | 191 |
| C314 | 6C6; P-2 | 193-194 |
| C312 | 6C4; P-1 | 195 |
| C317 | 6D3; P-1 | 197-198 |

| CDX Tasksheet Number | 2017 MAST NATEF Reference and Priority | Corresponding Page(s) |
| --- | --- | --- |
| C315 | 6D1; P-1 | 199 |
| C319 | 6D5; P-1 | 201-202 |
| C316 | 6D2; P-1 | 203-204 |
| C318 | 6D4; P-1 | 205 |
| C564 | 6E4; P-2 | 207 |
| C321 | 6E3; P-2 | 209 |
| C325 | 6F2; P-2 | 211-212 |
| C646 | 6F1; P-2 | 213-214 |
| C1003 | 6F3; P-2 | 215-216 |
| C320 | 6E1; P-1 | 217-218 |
| C956 | 6E2; P-1 | 219-220 |
| C336 | 6G3; P-3 | 221-222 |
| C827 | 7B4; P-2 | 223-224 |
| C866 | 7D8; P-2 | 225 |
| C566 | 7A9; P-3 | 227 |
| C376 | 7D4; P-3 | 229 |
| C865 | 7D5; P-3 | 231 |
| C362 | 7C3; P-2 | 233 |
| C378 | 7D6; P-1 | 235 |
| C373 | 7D1; P-1 | 237-238 |
| C374 | 7D2; P-2 | 239-240 |
| C835 | 7D3; P-2 | 241 |